Tools and Traits
for Highly Effective
Science Teaching,
K–8

Tools and Traits for Highly Effective Science Teaching, K–8

Jo Anne Vasquez, PhD

Heinemann
Portsmouth, NH

Heinemann
A division of Reed Elsevier Inc.
361 Hanover Street
Portsmouth, NH 03801–3912
www.heinemann.com

Offices and agents throughout the world

The author and publisher wish to thank those who have generously given permission to reprint borrowed material:

Figures 4.1–4.3: "Cookie Crumbles" probe, examples of student responses by Keeley, P., F. Eberle, and L. Farrin from *Uncovering Student Ideas in Science* (Vol.1, 2005). Reprinted by permission of NSTA Press.

Library of Congress Cataloging-in-Publication Data
Vasquez, Jo Anne.
    Tools and traits for highly effective science teaching, K–8 / Jo Anne Vasquez.
       p. cm.
    Includes bibliographical references and index.
    ISBN-13: 978-0-325-01100-4
    1. Science-Study and teaching (Elementary).   2. Science-Study and teaching (Middle school).
3. Elementary school teaching.   4. Middle school teaching.   5. Effective teaching.   I. Title.
    LB1585.V336 2008
    372.3'5—dc22   2007026778

Editor: Robin Najar
Production coordinator: Elizabeth Valway
Production service: Appingo Publishing Services
Cover design: Bernadette Skok
Composition: Appingo Publishing Services
Manufacturing: Jamie Carter

Printed in the United States of America on acid-free paper
11 10 09 08 07 VP 1 2 3 4 5

There is always a moment in childhood,
when the door opens and lets the future in!
Thanks to all those elementary teachers who spend
everyday nurturing our future.

Contents

Foreword

In January 2002 the most comprehensive federal education law ever written, No Child Left Behind (NCLB), was signed into law to ensure that schools would improve the achievement of all students. Embedded within this law is the notion of focusing on "what works" in improving teaching and learning by moving beyond anecdotes and opinions to the serious use of research or evidence-based programs. Coupled with this is the requirement for teachers to be highly qualified, which means that at a minimum, teachers in core subject areas must have a bachelor's degree, have full state certification, and demonstrate subject matter competency. However, the law itself does not describe how highly qualified translates into highly effective nor does it translate research into practice.

Moving beyond the minimum and sometimes vague requirements of the law has been particularly challenging for elementary teachers of science who may meet the designation of "highly qualified" but struggle with being an effective teacher of science. Furthermore, the NCLB's focus on reading and mathematics has diminished the importance of science and delayed the significant body of research on science teaching and learning in reaching where it matters most—our schools and classrooms.

At last, we have a comprehensive resource that can help teachers, administrators, and anyone who deeply cares about the science learning of our children move beyond the rhetoric of NCLB to help elementary teachers become both "highly qualified" and "highly effective" teachers of science. The comprehensive synthesis provided by Jo Anne Vasquez is particularly timely as NCLB science testing begins to take hold in our nation's schools, and elementary science gains the important place it deserves in the school curriculum. Also, the call for research-based practices has never been as strong as it is now. This is a book that blends the significant body of research and consensus thinking about high quality science education with practical advice culled from Jo Anne's many years as a highly respected and knowledgeable leader in elementary science education. Finally, teachers and administrators can "see" what effective elementary science teaching and learning looks like in the elementary classroom and acquire the tools and resources they need to build the capacity for schools to be highly effective in ensuring that all students have opportunities to become science literate.

Jo Anne artfully moves between specific applications of highly effective teaching to helping the reader connect these applications to the bigger picture of science teaching and learning. She begins by making a convincing case for why "highly qualified" is not synonymous with "highly effective" and takes the reader on a journey to uncover the myriad considerations one must take into account for improving the science literacy of both elementary teachers and their students.

The journey begins by helping the reader uncover the essence of inquiry, a centerpiece of elementary science teaching and learning. Through the interweaving of theory and practice, Jo Anne choreographs the "whats, hows, and whys" of promoting learning through inquiry-based practices known to work. She skillfully moves the reader beyond the common interpretation of inquiry as "hands-on science" to an understanding of inquiry as a set of abilities, understandings, and teaching methods that have rigorous and appropriate content at its core. As Jo Anne grounds the reader in the essential attributes of inquiry and the validity of inquiry-based teaching, she seamlessly inserts practical examples and authentic voices from the field to consider what it looks like in the classroom and the impact on student learning.

The journey continues by connecting elementary science with literacy development. In an NCLB world where literacy takes center stage, Jo Anne helps the reader understand the critical connection between science and language literacy. She makes a compelling case, supported by research, for why and how science provides a rich context in which to apply and practice literacy skills while at the same time building students' understanding of the natural world and teachers' understanding of science as a unique and important discipline.

In order for learning to take place, teachers and administrators need to understand the critical role formative assessment plays in the science program. At the heart of this is the importance of recognizing that students come to the science classroom with preconceived notions about how the natural world works. Being an effective elementary science teacher requires knowing how children think about science concepts, recognizing common misconceptions, and having strategies for challenging such misconceptions. Jo Anne provides a rich collection of research-based strategies, illustrative examples of student work and thinking, and resources for uncovering students' ideas and using them to build a bridge between their preconceptions and the scientific ideas we want them to understand and use throughout their lives.

Curriculum, assessment, and instruction are inextricably intertwined. This book describes resources and practical strategies for translating elementary science curricular standards and learning goals into practice by deeply understanding the content, teaching considerations for identifying, and implementing a coherent sequence of science instruction. The diversity of students in the science classroom may be regarded as the most important consideration of all in ensuring effective science teaching, Jo Anne brings all considerations for effective teaching full circle to view them through the lens of supporting the diverse needs of *all* learners. The reader comes to understand how *all* students' opportunities to learn should be characterized by differentiated opportunities to engage in the joy of learning science and how the entire classroom environment should be oriented toward a disposition of curiosity that challenges and contributes to every student's intellectual growth.

I applaud Jo Anne's tireless work in bringing all of these considerations and components of effective elementary science teaching together into a resource that respects the desire of teachers to provide the very best science education for their students and supports administrators who have the will and leadership to make this happen. This is a must-read book for everyone who cares deeply about education and the success of our students in facing a future that increasingly depends on a science literate citizenry. This book should be high on every elementary science stakeholder's reading list as an important reference for seeking deeper understanding of what it means to effectively teach elementary science. There is no idea or suggestion in this book that has not been tried, tested, and true in successful elementary science classrooms. The challenge for you, the elementary teacher, is to make the ideas in this book come alive in your classroom. The challenge for you, the administrator, is to engage and support all teachers of science in finding an inspirational path that leads toward effective science teaching. The challenge for you, the staff developer or facilitator of professional learning communities, is to integrate these components into teachers' learning. The final determinant of success in our collective efforts to ensure a quality elementary science education will be measured not just by NCLB mandated tests, but more importantly by the bright lights in the eyes of students who are captivated by a highly effective science teacher in a classroom where all students are learning at high levels.

—Page Keeley
Senior Science Program Director
Maine Mathematics and Science Alliance

Introduction

Over the past few decades the role of science in our everyday lives has increased significantly. As the advances in science and technology have changed the way we live, work, and even teach, it has created both conveniences and burdens. Educating today's students to live and work in this knowledge-based society will take teachers who ever increasingly think about their own science literacy as well as how they will provide experiences which will enable all students to become scientifically literate citizens.

All students, state the National Science Education Standards, "... will need to be able to use scientific information to make choices that arise every day. Everyone must be able to engage intelligently in public discourse and debate about important issues that involve science and technology. Everyone deserves to share in the excitement and personal fulfillment that can come from understanding and learning about the natural world." For this to happen, the role of an effective elementary teacher of science must take on a renewed importance in every school system. As the nation now moves toward the testing of science, how science will be taught is as important as what is going to be taught.

There is now an emerging body of knowledge in cognitive science which helps us understand how students learn, not only science but all subjects. This, coupled with effective and proven pedagogically approaches, can help all teachers become effective science instructors. This book is a practical attempt to pull upon this research and organize it in a way that will help elementary teachers of science, science supervisors, administrators and parents to recognize the traits of effective practice. In this book we will explore the following questions: How do you structure lessons, from providing inquiry-oriented lessons, using effective questions to probe children's thinking, to seamless formative assessment? What is effective integration and what is it not? How do you manage activity-based learning? How do we provide for all students within our classrooms?

In no way is this book attempting to provide the depth needed for each of these areas, but it will provide a primer or a place for teachers to start to think about issues such as, "Am I effectively teaching science? How can I become a more effective teacher?," while administrators can get a glimpse at the strategies and resources elementary teachers need in order to effectively teach inquiry-based science.

Tools and Traits
for Highly Effective
Science Teaching,
K–8

CHAPTER

1

What Effective Teachers of Science Know and Are Able To Do. What Does the Research Say?

Highly Qualified Versus Highly Effective: Is There a Difference?

The Federal No Child Left Behind Act of 2001 (NCLB) introduced both the concepts of "adequate yearly progress," based on annual testing, and "highly qualified teacher," based on teacher credentials. According to the legislation, "highly qualified" teachers are defined as those who hold at least a bachelor's degree, are fully licensed and credentialed in the state in the subjects they teach, and can demonstrate competence in the subjects they teach. While all of these indicators are significant, these factors do not necessarily define effectiveness. Highly effective teachers are able to envision instructional goals for their students, and then draw upon their knowledge and training to help students achieve success. A "highly qualified teacher" of science is a good place to begin. However, it is more important to have a teacher who is "highly effective," a teacher whose effort will yield high rates of student learning and performance. Fortunately or unfortunately, we are in an era of accountability, and part of this accountability will be determined by student performance on science assessments.

Dr. William Sanders, formerly at the University of Tennessee's Value-Added Research and Assessment Center, has provided research on the cumulative effect of teacher effectiveness on student achievement. Over a multiyear period, Sanders focused on what happened to students whose teachers produced low achievement results. His finding discovered children placed with three high-performing teachers in a row beginning in third grade, they scored on average at the 96th percentile on Tennessee's statewide mathematics assessment at the end of the fifth grade. When children with comparable achievement histories were placed with three low-performing teachers in a row beginning in third grade, their average score on the same mathematics assessment was at the 44th percentile, a 52-percentile point difference for children who presumably had comparable abilities and skills.

Similar findings come from a comparable study of math and reading in the early grades by researchers in Dallas, Texas. The average performance on the math section of the Iowa Tests of Basic Skills by students who were placed with three high performing teachers in a row increased from the 63rd to the 87th percentile. This is in contrast to their peers who had similar initial scores and whose performance decreased from the 58th to the 40th percentile, a difference of 44 percentile points (Wright, Horn, and Sanders 1997). These studies in Tennessee and Texas give credence to the idea that "the teacher makes the difference," and point out that the quality of the teacher and the teacher's effectiveness makes a big difference as well (Tucker and Stronge 2005).

The Education Policy Analysis Archives report *National Board Certification as Professional Development: What Are Teachers Learning?* (Lustick and Sykes 2006) presents evidence that through the process of becoming Board Certified, teachers facilitate greater student achievement; however, very little quantitative evidence exists to indicate how and to what extent the certification process improved teacher quality or effectiveness. The study does present evidence about what teachers are learning from the National Board Certification process. This evidence suggests teachers learn to be more reflective practitioners. As they become more aware of their own cognitive processes and their teaching strategies, the hypothesis is that as the quality of their teaching increases, it will enhance their students' learning. In addition to becoming a reflective practitioner, this report also points to two other areas of teacher growth: the ability to use scientific inquiry and the use of assessment to improve their instruction.

The strategies employed by National Board Certified teachers that promoted effective learning by their students include having students take an "active role" in their learning by arranging frequent opportunities for "hands-on" science activities and "open-ended investigations" complete with post-activity time for reflection and analysis. Teachers' understandings of scientific inquiry was reflected in the choices and decisions made in their planning, lesson management, and assessment. Teachers who chose age- and skill-level-appropriate classroom activities that were as much minds on as hands-on, and appropriate higher order questioning style, wait time, and discussion management were deemed highly effective (Lustick and Sykes 2006).

What Are Some General Qualities of Effective Teachers?

Like all of us, teachers have many early school memories about how science was taught to them. These memories can carry over into their own classroom practice. Often the lessons learned include "teaching is telling," "to learn is to memorize," and "content is disconnected" (Lederman, Gess-Hewsome, and Latz 1994) Unfortunately, university method classes often reinforce these early experiences, and as a result elementary teachers come into teaching presenting fragmented, superficial, and disconnected lessons. However, we all can look back into our own learning and remember the effective teachers who inspired us and helped us learn far beyond what it took to just pass the test. These effective teachers enriched our daily lives, helped shape our career aspirations, and, perhaps, inspired us to become life-long learners.

There seems to be a clear consensus on what effective teachers do to enhance student learning, and meta-analyses by researchers such as Marzano, Pickering, and Pollock (2001) have begun to quantify the average effects of specific instructional strategies. Clearly the research is pointing to a link between what the teacher knows about the content and the pedagogy and how the teacher articulates this knowledge into their classroom practice. The body of evidence for this effectiveness based on student achievement is much stronger in mathematics and reading because they are tested under NCLB, while evidence for effective science instruction, especially in elementary schools, is considerably less, because science in elementary schools is just now being tested. Therefore, to build the case for what makes a highly effective teacher of elementary science, we mainly have to rely on the research about what science educators know about enhancing and improving scientific literacy.

If we want effective science teachers to enhance students' scientific literacy, the teachers themselves must be scientifically literate. Based on the small body of research, this poses a barrier for the majority of elementary teachers. Because of training and education, the majority of elementary teachers in the K–5 or 6 classrooms are generalists in education, meaning they had perhaps one or two core science lab courses in pre-service preparation and then perhaps a semester course about science teaching methods. When thrust into the elementary classroom, most teachers feel less qualified to teach science than any other subject. This premise is largely based upon a recent survey by Horizon Research of elementary teachers that showed that 76 percent felt "well qualified" to teach reading and language arts, 60 percent felt this way for mathematics, 52 percent for social studies, 29 percent for life science, 25 percent for earth science, and 18 percent for physical science (Weiss 2005). Therefore, the vast majority of elementary teachers who now have to teach science as a requirement for NCLB lack the skills and knowledge necessary to be effective before they ever set foot before their students, and they are especially lacking in the skills and content knowledge necessary to teach the physical sciences. This research shows us that the first step in developing effective elementary science teachers is increasing the science literacy of the teachers themselves.

What Does It Mean for an Effective Teacher to Be Scientifically Literate?

What is science literacy and how literate does an elementary teacher have to be in order to become an effective practitioner? Although there is great debate among science educators and scientists as to what the term "scientifically literate" actually means, for us, in this context, the term implies a general knowledge and appreciation of the enterprise of science in all disciplines, an ability to critically read and understand basic science articles found in newspapers and magazines, and the ability to question what they hear on television or read on the internet. Basic science literacy is an essential element of an individual's role as a citizen in a democratic society. Achieving scientific literacy for all students in our democracy is even more critical than ever given our growing reliability on science and technology and all the problems and possibilities they provide for our future. For science education, literacy is the foundation, and the science standards, both national and state, provide the specifications and framework for what the students should know and be able to understand as they travel on the pathway to becoming scientifically literate citizens. Given all of this, for teachers to be scientifically literate, they must at least have the same level of literacy as their students.

What Do Effective Teachers Do Differently?

In the findings of the 2000 Policy Information Center report *How Teaching Matters: Bringing the Classroom Back Into Discussions of Teacher Quality* (Wenglinsky 2000), students learn more from "good" teachers than from "bad" teachers under virtually any set of circumstances, for example, class size, parent involvement, learning technology, and materials. The challenge to the findings in order to recommend policy changes was to define "good" teachers. In the simplest sense the study defined "good" teachers as those who seemed to know how to make students learn, and a "better," or what I would call "an effective" teacher was one who enabled the same or similar students to learn more because they encouraged and guided their students to become the facilitators of their own learning. To help identify these unknowns in regard to what the meaning of a good teacher is, this study was a first attempt (using a national database and sophisticated analytical techniques) to answer the question of whether effective teachers do things differently in their classrooms.

In analyzing the data of a little more than seven thousand eighth-grade students who took the National Assessment of Educational Progress (NAEP) math and science tests, it was possible to relate various aspects of teacher quality to student test scores, while taking into account other potential influences on these scores, such as class size and students' social background. Although this study looked at eighth-grade students who took the NAEP math and science assessments, it clearly begins, in general terms, to describe a picture of effective teachers nationally. Teacher content knowledge, education level, and teaching experience were indeed factors in student achievement, but beyond this, some very clear indicators of effective classroom practice emerged:

- In both math and science, approximately half of all teachers had received more than two days of professional development within the past year.

- Cooperative learning strategies were the common topic used in professional development.

- In both math and science, teachers reported testing students at least once a month; these tests were more likely to require extended written answers than multiple-choice responses.

- Two out of three teachers engaged in hands-on learning activities with their students. Students of these teachers outperformed their peers by more than 40 percent above grade level in science and 70 percent above grade level in math.

- Students whose science teachers had received professional development in laboratory skills outperformed their peers by more than 40 percent of a grade level.

- Students whose teachers had received professional development in working with special populations outperformed their peers by more than a full grade level.

- Students whose teachers had received professional development in higher-order thinking skills outperformed their peers by 40 percent of a grade level.

- Teachers who administered point-in-time tests are associated with higher student performance than on-going techniques, such as portfolio or project-based assessment. Students outperformed by 46 percent of a grade level in math and 92 percent of a grade level in science. (The author notes this finding does not suggest portfolio assessments should be entirely supplanted by multiple choice tests, but rather that both are important to show student growth, although extended written responses are the most effective.)

This study provides a picture of supportive practices that will lead to effective science teaching. Certainly it shows that a great indicator of improving classroom practice is professional development opportunities for:

- developing higher-order thinking skills,
- conducting hands-on learning activities,
- relying on tests to help monitor student progress,
- learning to work with special populations,
- learning effective strategies for helping students learn concepts and then apply them to various situations,
- providing strategies for individualizing instruction, and
- helping to increase their own content knowledge.

Is Knowledge of Both Content and Scientific Process Necessary for Effective Practice?

Learning is not necessarily an outcome of teaching. Many teachers provide instruction that helps students recognize that the sun is the center of our solar system and the earth revolves around it, or that gravity is the force that holds us on Earth. They believe a good student of science should be able to reproduce this information as accurately as possible, thus it helped students understand *what scientists know*. Teachers may even have the students design experiments where they form a hypothesis, conduct their test, and write their conclusions, thus giving their students hands-on experience using the scientific process, or experience acting out *how scientists know*. Providing students with the "how" and the "know" is not necessarily an incorrect way to teach science. However, based on the research literature synthesized in the National Research Council's report *How Students Learn Science in the Classroom* (NRC 2005, 468–69), we now know that teachers need to move students beyond the "know" (content matter) and the "how" (using the scientific method or the process) to the development of: 1) a familiarity with science concepts, theories, and models; 2) an understanding of how knowledge is generated and justified; and 3) an ability to use these understandings to engage in new inquiry.

Teachers who teach using the "how" and "know" experiences for their students are not necessarily ineffective teachers. However, they are at the beginning or *novice stage* of the teaching of science, and many will not move beyond this level! What we want is to help elementary teachers understand and recognize that their students' come to them with existing preconceptions about science phenomena. Simply having them do the scientific method is not sufficient for conceptual change. Teachers must help students develop the knowledge, skills, and attitudes that will enable them to understand what it means to "do science" and participate in a larger scientific community. In other words, if these students are going to be successful in this ever-changing, "flat" world, then they will need to develop the skills of learning how to learn, adopt their own questioning stance, and be able to search for both supporting and conflicting evidence—hallmarks of the scientific enterprise.

There are three guiding principles effective teachers of science have in common. They are the ability to:

- recognize and probe for students' preconceptions based on their everyday experiences and intuitive notions,

- understand what it means to "do science," and

- provide opportunities for students to take a metacognitive approach to learning.

Beyond these three guiding principles, effective teachers of science have classrooms that are learner-centered, knowledge-centered, assessment-centered, and community-centered.

All teaching is an art, a craft that is honed over time through professional growth experiences, self-reflection, and professional practice. Teachers with sustained professional development will also:

- have a deep understanding of the content and concepts they are teaching;

- understand standards-based instruction;

- provide developmentally appropriate, interesting instruction that is relevant to their students' lives;

- provide active, engaging activities that encourage discourse in the classroom;

- provide more student responsibility and choice;

- employ a blend of teaching strategies, including inquiring, problem solving, conjecturing, inventing, producing, and finding answers;

- accommodate individual student needs, whether cultural, developmental, or cognitive;

- infuse a multicultural perspective where appropriate; and

- make connections across the curriculum. (Weiss 2005)

In order for teachers to become skilled at teaching in an inquiry-oriented manner as outlined in *How Students Learn: Science in the Classroom* (National Research Council 2005), they need to develop the necessary skills over time to be able to adjust their lessons to fit the stage of inquiry needed to make certain the student masters the concept. Highly effective teachers of science will be able to construct their lessons using strategies from student-initiated inquiry to a more guided or structured activity. These activities need to be combined with class discussion, writing in science notebooks, reading, researching, solving problems, and activities that develop students' problem-solving skills. The key to effective practice for teachers is that they identify the intended learning outcome, design appropriate learning experiences, and effectively assess the students' progress (National Research Council 2005).

Learning what it means to engage in scientific inquiry provides teachers with the base to develop learning experiences from first-hand, concrete experiences to the more distant or abstract. Teaching through an inquiry approach requires students to do more than observe, infer, and experiment. It requires them to combine scientific processes with content knowledge and use critical thinking skills and scientific reasoning to develop a deep understanding of science (National Research Council 1996). This type of learning can be accomplished in the context of many different specific topics. Unlike mathematics, where topics such as whole-number arithmetic are foundational for the study of rational numbers, there is little agreement on the selection and sequencing of specific topics in science, particularly at the elementary level. What is clearly foundational for later science study is learning what it means to engage in scientific inquiry.

Helping their students engage in scientific inquiry to develop scientific knowledge often requires teachers to provide experiences, which students may not otherwise directly experience in their everyday lives. This is when students develop conceptualized aspects of the world. For instance, the study of light gives children an accessible opportunity to view the world differently and challenge their existing conceptions. We see the world around us because light reflects from objects to our eyes, and yet we do not sense that what we see is the result of reflected light. A highly effective teacher of science will know and understand the conceptual development that is required by their students to grasp such concepts and will provide experiences for their students to develop this major conceptual leap.

Effective teachers of science are able to connect assessment, curriculum, and teaching as a system consistent with the principles of *How People Learn* (National Research Council 1999). There will be a flow to the way they teach, which will be student-centered, knowledge-centered, and assessment-centered. There is support for the fact that effective teachers not only make students feel good about school and learning, but also their work articulates into higher student achievement. Although the studies on effective science teaching in the elementary classroom are not plentiful, the common indicators clearly point to teachers needing high levels of verbal ability, deep content knowledge, pedagogical knowledge, certification status, ability to use a wide range of teaching strategies skillfully, and enthusiasm about the subject area (Darling-Hammond 2000).

References

American Association for the Advancement of Science. 1993. *Benchmarks for Science Literacy.* Washington, DC: AAAS Press.

Darling-Hammond, L. 2000. *Teacher Quality and Student Achievement: A Review of State Policy Evidence.* Education Policy Analysis Archives, 8(1).

Lederman, N., J. Gess-Newsome, and M. Latz. 1994. "The Nature and Development of Preservice Science Teachers' Conceptions of Subject Matter and Pedagogy." *Journal of Research in Science Teaching*, 31, 129–46.

Lustick, D., and G. Sykes. 2006. National Board Certification as Professional Development: What are Teachers Learning? Education Policy Analysis Achives, 14 (5). http://epaa.asu.edu/epaa/v15n5/

National Research Council. 2005. *How Students Learn: Science in the Classroom.* Washington, DC: National Academy Press.

National Research Council. 1999. *How People Learn: Bridging Research to Practice.* Washington, DC: National Academy Press.

National Research Council. 1999. *How People Learn: Brain, Mind, Experience, and School.* Washington, DC: National Academy Press.

National Research Council. 1996. *National Science Education Standards.* Washington, DC: National Academy of Science.

Sanders, W. L., and J. C. Rivers. 1996. *Cumulative and Residual Effects of Teachers on Future Student Academic Achievement.* (Research Progress Report.) Knoxville, TN: University of Tennessee Value-Added Research and Assessment Center.

Tucker, P. D., and J. H. Stronge. 2005. *Linking Teacher Evaluation and Student Learning.* Alexandria, VA: Association for Supervision and Curriculum Development.

Weiss. I. 2005. *Research on Effective Professional Development.* Chapel Hill, NC: Horizon Research, Inc.

Wenglinsky, H. 2000. *How Teaching Matters: Bringing the Classroom Back Into Discussions of Teacher Quality.* Princeton, NJ: Education Testing Service.

Wright, S. P., S. P. Horn, and W. L. Sanders. 1997. "Teacher and Classroom Context Effects on Student Achievement: Implication for Teacher Evaluations." *Journal of Personnel Evaluation in Education* 11: 57–67.

CHAPTER

2

What is Inquiry Science?

Scientific inquiry has it roots in the human mind. Humans are inherently curious creatures and for millennia we have asked, "Why does it do that?" In societies where inquiry has flourished, so has human progress. Questioning and debate have helped great civilizations develop. In fifth-century-B.C. Athens, one of humankind's most celebrated inquiry teachers, Socrates, challenged the youth to think for themselves, to question the wisdom of their elders, and to probe the unsolved mysteries of the natural world. So too throughout history great masters, including Plato, Aristotle, Galileo, and Leonardo, dared to question and find out for themselves. The great discoveries started with observations and moved to questioning in the pursuit of answers.

John Dewey, a twentieth-century educator and philosopher, made a persuasive case for the importance of inquiry-based teaching as a way of preserving values in a world threatened by totalitarianism. He argued that the scientific method is the only authentic means at our command for getting at the significance of our everyday experiences of the world in which we live. He strongly felt and wrote that the ability to reason scientifically is an essential skill for coping with the complexities of modern life, and he warned that failure to cultivate this skill risked a return to intellectual and moral authoritarianism. If only John Dewey could get a glimpse of the world students live in today, where they are bombarded with the information that we so strongly feel the need to impart upon them. While children need to learn content knowledge, it must be learned in a meaningful way that will engage students and cultivate their own natural curiosity. In order to become a creative, innovative thinker one has to engage in the processes of science. This activity is the same whether you are a research scientist or a kindergarten student. It all starts with a journey into the inquiry process: "I wonder why it does that?"

Do It With Me, Not To Me!

Activity for experience

"Keeping children busy, physically active, is not the criterion for effective science teaching. Activity must be a vehicle for experience and thought, and thought is promoted by communication and discussion. The teacher's role in this process is crucial to the children's learning." (Harlen 2001, 8)

Consider a classroom in which the students are gathered around a long table where many different items are laid out. There are several glass soda bottles filled to different heights with colored water, a small xylophone, an open shoe box surrounded with different sizes of rubber bands, a pair of maracas, a bell from a bicycle, and even a wooden flute. The teacher has planned a third-grade lesson about sound. She begins by saying, "I want you to close your eyes and be very quiet. I want you to listen." After a minute, which is about as long as the students can stand being quiet, she asks them to tell her what they heard. The students respond by describing the sound of the gurgling pump in their fish tank, the hum of the computers lined up against one side of the room, footsteps of students walking by, and even, "I think I hear my heart beating in my ears."

This incredible teacher has begun to take her students on a journey of inquiry involving the elements of sound, their own hearing and listening skills, how sound is produced, and how sound can be changed. She is a highly skilled elementary teacher who has honed the art of inquiry science teaching over several years. She knows that it involves practice and preparation and goes beyond standing and delivering information about sound, or having her students just read about sound. It involves them discovering for themselves the elements of sounds. She knows that children have a sense of wonder and curiosity and if this is not fostered at a very young age, science will become "just another body of knowledge to learn in order to pass the test."

A teacher's ability to do inquiry-based science in the elementary classroom takes practice, preparation, and a well-developed series of professional development experiences. Some teachers enter the profession with a natural ability to engage their students, perhaps because they had teachers themselves who engaged them in inquiry-based teaching. Teachers who do so, however, are few and far between. Most of the best teachers of inquiry have worked hard to develop their craft.

Nancy Chesley pretty much sums up the essence of the elements of inquiry that we will now examine in this chapter.

Inquiry Science—A Three-Legged Stool

The National Science Education Standards (National Research Council 1996) and the companion book *Inquiry and the National Science Education Standards* (NRC 2000), lay the foundation for developing students' science literacy. Becoming a scientifically literate person requires the ability to do and an understanding of scientific inquiry.

These two documents talk about the three legs of the inquiry stool. The first is the students' *ability* to do scientific inquiry. This is when a student can ask questions, plan and conduct a simple investigation, use equipment, communicate their results and modify their explanations. This is what we refer to as *doing science*.

The second is the students' *understanding* of scientific inquiry. This is when students understand how and why scientific knowledge changes in response to new evidence, logical analysis, and modified explanations debated within a community of scientists. The debate about the planet Pluto is an excellent example of this. This is how students identify the true nature of science as an evolving body of knowledge. It is this knowing how to do science and understanding the enterprise of science that fosters science literacy.

This brings us to the third leg of the inquiry stool: *inquiry as a set of teaching methods the teachers can use.* This helps guide teachers as they plan lessons that will promote the students' *abilities to do scientific inquiry* and their *understanding of scientific inquiry*. For example, this is demonstrated in how teachers set up their investigations, how they provide the students access to the content of science, how they ask questions to probe students' thinking, and how they adapt their curricula to meet the interests, knowledge, understanding, and experience of their students. Science educators understand inquiry is not the only way to teach. However, it needs to be the central part of an effective teacher's lessons. Some teachers say, "I teach using hands-on." However, hands-on does not guarantee inquiry is taking place.

"I Taught My Students How to Do the Scientific Method and They Are Good at Using It!"

Rodger Bybee [handwritten note in margin]

In his book *Learning Science and the Science of Learning*, Rodger Bybee describes the key elements of scientific inquiry as "observation, hypothesis, inference, test, and feedback." He goes on to say, "All of these processes serve the end of obtaining and using empirical evidence to help answer a scientific question" (Bybee 2002, 27). You may have heard this referred to as the "scientific method."

Some teachers call the *doing* of inquiry science the "scientific method." Dr. Bybee describes inquiry teaching as a much deeper process than just the lock-step procedure often associated with this term. It is true that students will engage in the process of answering a question through a series of investigations that will lead them to engage in what is called the "scientific method." But the difference between an inquiry approach used by a skilled teacher is the path they develop for the student to follow, the level of engagement of the teacher along this path, and the engagement of the student at these different levels. Science educators have moved away from saying "scientific method" because it implies this lock-step approach without regard to the thinking or the process the students use in their investigation. Instead the more accepted term is "scientific process," implying students' engagement in the act or process of scientific investigation.

The first thing teachers need to recognize is the ability and skills of their students for the level they are teaching. Setting up an experimental designed investigation is not appropriate for primary students as there are a set of skills and abilities they need to develop in order to move to a higher level where this is appropriate. The problem with today's educational climate is that most of the primary science investigations have been eliminated, giving those students at intermediate levels no foundation on which to build. If teachers chose to skip addition and subtraction in primary grades and skip to multiplication in third grade, the students would fail. This is somewhat the same as the developmental building of the student's understandings and abilities in primary.

The following chart compares the inquiry abilities of students in grades K–4 with those of students in grades 5–8 (National Research Council 1966, 122, 145, 148). A skilled teacher will recognize that students' inquiry abilities reflect their cognitive development, and will use these for their level of engagement.

In grades K–4 students are expected to "employ simple equipment and tools to gather data," while students in grades 5–8 should also be able to "analyze and interpret data." In grades K–4 students should be able to "use data to construct reasonable explanations," while in grades 5–8 students should be able to "recognize and analyze alternative explanations and predictions." Effective teachers will recognize that instruction on

Figure 2–1

Abilities Necessary for Scientific Inquiry	
Grades K–4 Abilities Necessary for Scientific Inquiry	Grades 5–8 Abilities Necessary for Scientific Inquiry
Ask a question about objects, organisms, and events in the environment.	Identify questions that can be answered through scientific investigations.
Plan and conduct a simple investigation.	Design and conduct a scientific investigation.
Employ simple equipment and tools to gather data and extend the senses.	Use appropriate tools and techniques to gather, analyze, and interpret data.
Use data to construct a reasonable explanation.	Develop descriptions, explanations, predictions, and models using evidence.
	Think critically and logically to establish the relationship between evidence and explanations.
	Recognize and analyze alternative explanations and predictions.
Communicate investigations and explanations.	Communicate scientific procedures and explanations.
	Use mathematics in all aspects of scientific inquiry.

inquiry abilities in isolation of science content is totally ineffective. Both science content and the process or *doing* science is needed in inquiry-based instruction. One without the other does not provide the skills necessary for the student to become scientifically literate. In other words, a balanced approach is needed.

Are Different Levels of Engagement Needed between the Teacher and the Student?

Science educators, textbooks, and professional developers toss out many terms that can be very confusing to elementary teachers. You may hear, for example, that the teaching of inquiry can be open, full, partial, structured, guided, or directed. These terms are even showing up in science textbooks' activities labels to show they are "inquiry-oriented": they can be very confusing, even to science educators. However, a commonly held belief presented clearly in *Inquiry, and the National Science Education Standards* is that highly effective teachers will employ a range of strategies to move their students along a continuum to develop a range of abilities to engage in science inquiry. They likely move from a guided or directed instructional approach to an open or student-initiated approach.

The following chart demonstrates that inquiry-based teaching varies in degree of structure and guidance by teachers and/or by the materials they are using.

Figure 2–2

Essential Features of Classroom Inquiry and Their Variations				
Essential Feature	Level I	Level II	Level III	Level IV
1. Learner engages in scientifically oriented question(s)	Learner engages with question(s) provided by teacher, materials, or other source	Learner sharpens or clarifies question provided by teacher, materials, or other source	Learner selects from among questions, modifying as necessary	Learner poses own questions
2. Learner participates in design of *procedures* for gathering evidence	Learner is given procedures to follow	Learner clarifies or modifies procedures for gathering evidence	Learner is guided in designing own procedures for gathering evidence	Learner designs own procedures for gathering evidence
3. Learner gives priority to *evidence* in responding to questions	Learner is given data and told how to analyze	Learner is given data and asked to analyze	Learner is directed to collect certain data and asked to analyze	Learner determines what constitutes evidence and collects it
4. Learner formulates *explanations* from evidence	Learner is provided with explanation	Learner is given possible ways to use evidence to formulate explanation	Learner is guided in process of formulating explanations from evidence	Learner formulates explanation based upon evidence
5. Learner connects explanations to scientific knowledge	Learner makes no connection to scientific knowledge	Learner is given possible connections to scientific knowledge	Learner is directed toward sources of scientific knowledge and asked to make connections	Learner independently connects explanations and scientific knowledge
6. Learner communicates and justifies explanations	Learner is given steps and procedures for communication	Learner is provided with broad guidelines to use and sharpen communication	Learner is coached in development of communication	Learner forms reasonable and logical argument to communicate own explanations

Less ....Amount of Learner Self-Direction ....More

More ....Amount of Direction from Teacher or Material...................................Less

(National Research Council, Inquiry and the National Science Education Standards 2000, 29)

A skilled teacher of science will be able to move between the different variations in the amount of structure, guidance, and coaching they give their students. For the purpose of this discussion, the terms of structured, guided, and open or (student-initiated) are used here (Jarrett 1997).

- On left end will be a very low-level or *structured-inquiry* lesson where the teacher directs and models with specific focus the goal or outcome of the investigation. These are often more of the "cookbook" lock-step lessons found in my classrooms. The students are engaged; however, they follow a prescribed set of directions.

- In the middle, the teachers facilitate or provide a *guided-inquiry* experience with greater responsibility for the process given to the students as they take responsibility for determining procedures for investigation. The teacher may still be suggesting the questions to investigate.

- At the right end is more *open* or *student-initiated inquiry* where the students have the most responsibility as they generate their own questions and design their own investigations.

The far right-hand side with the more open or student-initiated inquiry is the most difficult for teachers to achieve due to their own skills and content knowledge and the availability of time. If the teacher is going from a structured lesson to the student-initiated or open lesson where the students set up their own investigations based on their questions, the teacher must provide time for this to happen, as well as materials and access to other information (the Web, resource books, etc.). The teacher who can provide an inquiry-oriented lesson from structured inquiry to open inquiry will help their students to develop the cognitive and meta-cognitive skills necessary to be successfully scientifically literate. However, to achieve this level of inquiry, students much first learn to ask and evaluate questions that can be investigated, understand the difference between the evidence and their opinion, and develop a defensible explanation.

These phases or levels of inquiry instruction will have several different names. For the most part, however, science educators agree upon the intent and necessity of levels. Within classroom instruction the use of open or student-initiated inquiry investigations will take more time and require a skilled professional who is willing and able to be the "guide-by-the-side" for their students. Usually such teachers have a deeper understanding of the content, know how to ask effective questions to promote higher-level thinking, and feel comfortable facilitating and entertaining the student's questions, even to the point of being able to say, "I don't know the answer, but why don't we see if we can find out together."

An experienced teacher will move through these three phases of inquiry instruction knowing there are times when the low-level structured activities are necessary to meet a specific goal and/or given the amount of class time. Employing all phases of inquiry instruction also provides opportunities for all students to have the same learning experience. I have heard some highly skilled teachers say, "It levels the playfield for all the students and helps me see where their misconceptions are emerging." As students move through the levels they take ownership of the investigation and begin to channel their activities into investigatable questions.

The following is a short example of an investigation that moves from teacher-directed to student-initiated.

Question to Investigate: How Can You Make Sound?

Materials

Clear straws, scissors, and tape.

Teacher poses the question to the class and then takes responses and records them on a chart. Responses show how many the students already know about sound, movement of air, vibrations, etc.

Structured Inquiry:

Teacher "Blow through the straw. What do you hear?"

Students respond by blowing air through the straw. The air makes a sound.

Teacher "Let's see if we can make this straw into an instrument. Flatten the straw on one end, then cut a point in the shape of an upside down V. Then flatten the straw some more. Now try and blow through the straw. What do you hear?"

Students "It tickled my lips." "It moved my lips." "I felt it tingle my lips."

Teacher "What is different about our straw from before? What can you say about how we can now make a noise as the air moves through?"

Students will be able to identify that the sound is happening because the straw is moving where it is cut. Therefore the teacher will now list conditions to produce sound: Something causing the air to move back and forth. It takes a motion to move something.

Guided Inquiry:

Teacher "What would happen if you changed your straw in some way to make a different sound? Can you think of ways to do this? Make a prediction about what the sound might be like." (Students are given several choices and not told what to do. However, they are now directed toward the ways sound can change by the length of the straw or by adding another straw to it, putting holes into the straw, etc.)

Teacher "Can you demonstrate your sound? What did you discover about the length? What did you discover about adding holes? How do you think sound changes?"

Students will recognize that by changing their straws they are able to change the "pitch." The main outcomes are that the students begin to recognize that sound is made when an object vibrates and that sound can be changed by the design of the object. Formal language is not necessary during this time. However, if students do bring it up, it is good to list this on the chart.

Student-Initiated Inquiry

Teacher "What other questions do you have about sound? Can you think of ways you can test your questions, or are there other ways to find out the answers to your questions?"

Students are given the opportunity to brainstorm some more questions they might have about sound. In some cases they may have been questions the students asked during the prior experiences and the teacher has recorded them on a chart for later reference. Students might ask questions such as "How does sound travel? How far will it travel?" or "Will the sound be louder if it travels through water or my desk top?" These questions could be answered by setting up an investigation. However, some questions the students might have are answered by interviewing an expert or doing some research. For example, "Does our city have a sound ordinance? If so, how do they enforce it?" These are still good inquiry questions.

By moving along this continuum from guided to student-initiated investigation, the teacher is assuring that all students have a common experience and the beginning building of conceptual understanding is given to the students in a concrete way. This activity is a fairly easy one. However, when a more complex experiment is designed by the students, there is always the issue of time. Therefore many teachers will provide for the first two stages and might even set up a center for the last phase and/or skip it all together. But the caution here is not to skip the student-initiated inquiry phase, because this gives students the opportunity to apply their investigation skills.

What Are the Implications of Teaching Using an Inquiry Approach and How is Instruction Designed?

How People Learn (Bransford, Brown, and Cocking 1999) provides the research for the three fundamental and well-established principles of learning that will increase student understanding in science content and concept knowledge. Their findings show:

1. Teachers need to access student's prior knowledge about how the world works. If their initial understanding is not engaged, they may fail to grasp the new concepts and information. If not engaged, they may learn the information for the test but will revert to their preconceptions outside the classroom.

2. To develop competence in the area of inquiry, students must have a deep foundation of usable knowledge in the context of a conceptual framework and develop the ability to organize knowledge in ways that facilitate retrieval and application.

3. A meta-cognitive approach to instruction can help students learn to take control of their own learning by defining learning goals and monitoring their progress in achieving them.

When instruction takes place where these core principals of learning occur in the teaching and learning of science, essential features apply across all grade levels. *Inquiry and the National Science Education Standards* lay out five essential features (NRC 2000, 23–28). These five essential features, commonly called the 5-E instructional approach or the learning-cycle approach, have their theoretical foundations in the constructivist learning and teaching approach. This approach consists of the following phases: engagement, exploration, explanation, elaboration, and evaluation. According to Bybee (1997), "Each phase has a specific function and contributes to the coherent instruction and the increased student understanding of scientific and technological knowledge, attitudes and skills."

The 5-E instructional model helps teachers to frame their lessons into a sequence that provides adequate time and appropriate opportunities for conceptual change to occur. The 5-E instructional model also provides a framework with which they will build on their prior knowledge, and actively engage in doing science through investigations, which will then move them to a deeper conceptual understanding of science content by demonstrating their understanding through application and evaluation.

There are other models and constructs of the learning cycle, but the most widely accepted model among science educators is the 5-E. This instructional model is based upon the research of teaching and learning, plus it is consistent with current views of inquiry and inquiry teaching.

The chart Figure 2–1 provides a visual of this model. Clearly, it is not a linear approach but a cycle, which is the intent of its use.

How Does It Look When All the Inquiry Pieces Are Put Together to Support the Teaching and Learning of Science?

Figure 2–4 provides a glimpse of how the 5-E instruction model can be used to teach a concept.

Science concept: Properties of sound, such as pitch, can be changed by changing the properties of sound source that is, changing the rate of vibration.

Assessment: Students will demonstrate understanding by describing in their own words or creating an instrument to show how sound is produced and how pitch can be changed by changing the rate of vibration.

Figure 2–3   *5-E Instruction Model*

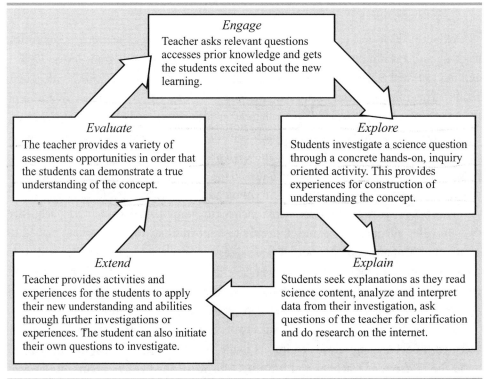

Figure 2–4

Instructional Phase	Teaching Strategies	Students' Actions
Engage	Teacher initiates the learning task, accesses prior knowledge, listens for students' misconceptions and sets the stage for the learning outcome by: ■ Asking questions showing pictures ■ Creating different sounds to elicit responses that uncover students' current knowledge about the how sound is produced ■ Listens and records words or terms the students already know	Shows students' interest in the topic by: ■ Describing past experiences with sound ■ Asking questions as different types of sounds are heard ■ Explaining in their own words they think sound is produced
Explore *Structured inquiry:* The students are shown how to make a straw flute with all given the same experience. *Guided inquiry:* The students are given a question but come up with their own ways to answer it. *Student-initiated inquiry* Students work in groups to answer their own questions. The teacher is now capturing the students' own language and terms for use during the debriefing time. This use of non-academic language will help students internalize the formal language of science.	Teacher provides a concrete experience by: ■ Asking the student a question, such as, "How can you make sound with a straw?" ■ Challenging with more open questions to investigate, "How can you make the sound change?" (They may add another straw, shorten the straw, put holes in the straw, etc.) ■ Providing students time to ask their own questions to investigate with the straw flute and/or allowing them to come up with other ways to make sound using what they have learned.	Students respond by: ■ Designing and testing their predictions and hypotheses ■ Forming new predictions and hypotheses to test ■ Recording their observations and ideas and work with others in their group to compare their findings ■ Beginning to think of new questions to investigate

continued

Figure 2–4

Instructional Phase	Teaching Strategies	Students' Actions
Explain	Teacher listens to the students' ideas about how sound is produced and changed, records their observations and explanations from their exploratory activities, and then prepares to explain the concept by: ■ Providing reference materials to read about how sound is produced, what causes pitch, and how sound travels ■ Providing formal definitions and introducing new vocabulary by referring to the students' own words used during the exploratory activities. ■ Providing opportunities for students to read and discuss with a partner (through pair-sharing) other information they find on sound	Students will begin to assimilate new understanding of sound by: ■ Referring to their own notes on observations from the exploratory activities ■ Reading material about sound that clarifies their understanding of new vocabulary (either alone or in a pair) ■ Listening to other students' explanations of the concept. ■ Asking other questions they may have about sound ■ Relating experiences from their own lives about the concept of how sound is produced
Extend	Teachers will provide other avenues for students to extend and apply the new learning through: ■ Creating opportunities for the students to create their own instruments, which will demonstrate how sound is made and how different pitches can be created. ■ Using new vocabulary in ways that will demonstrate understanding ■ Setting up investigations on how sound travels to our ear or making a string phone and explaining how sound is traveling ■ Providing information to read and learn about the parts of the ear and their functions in listening	The student will respond by: ■ Applying new information in different ways by investigating new question of their own about sound ■ Using their new information to create a poster or drawing that demonstrates understanding of the new concept ■ Bringing in different instruments to demonstrate how sound is produced ■ Researching how different animals hear sounds and how they differ from humans

continued

Figure 2–4

Instructional Phase	Teaching Strategies	Students' Actions
Evaluate	Teacher provides opportunities for students to demonstrate understanding by: ■ Asking different levels of questions ranging from low order, such as "What causes sound?" and "What happens when you loosen the string on a guitar?" to critical thinking, such as "You hear nothing but your dog is barking? What is happening?"	The student demonstrates understanding of the new concept by: ■ Answering different levels of question and using constructive responses rather than one-word answers ■ Operationally defining the new vocabulary ■ Making an instrument that shows how sound is produced and how pitch can be changed

Inquiry Cycle

The 5-E instruction model helps us to frame the teaching of a concept, but within the teaching of inquiry itself lies the inquiry cycle, which is where the students pose a testable question that they can answer on their own either through direct observation, by manipulating variables in an experimental setting, or further research and usually one question will lead to other questions to test and investigate. This is how a scientist works (Pearce 1999). Questions are the heart of inquiry teaching; looking at questions and questioning will be more fully covered in Chapter 4.

Summary Thoughts

When we talk about teachers being able to teach in an inquiry-oriented way, we are referring to something that is very complex and brings all of the tenets of inquiry together. This takes a highly skilled professional. However, the pieces of the inquiry structure, from the lesson design using the 5-E instructional model, to moving students from structured to student-initiated inquiry, can be mastered through professional development, coaching, mentoring, and classroom practice. When the standards—whether they are local, state, or national—call for science to be taught in an inquiry-oriented way, it is necessary for school leaders to recognize this is not something mastered overnight but is a bar for all elementary teachers to achieve.

References

Abell, Sandra, and M. Volkmann. 2006. *Seamless Assessment in Science.* Portsmouth, NH: Heine-
    mann.

Bransford, John, A. Brown, and R. Cocking, eds. 1999. *How People Learn: Brain, Mind, Experience,
    and School.* Washington, DC: National Academy Press.

Bybee, Rodger. 1997. *Achieving Scientific Literacy: From Purposes to Practices.*
Portsmouth, NH: Heinemann.

———. 2002. "Scientific Inquiry, Student Learning, and the Science Curriculum." *In Learning
    Science and Science of Learning,* edited by Rodger Bybee, 25–35. Arlington, VA: NSTA Press.

Dewey, John. 1938. *Experience and Education.* New York: Macmillan.

Harlen, Wynn. 2001. *Primary Science Taking the Plunge,* Second Edition. Portsmouth, NH: Heine-
    mann.

Jarret, Dennis. 1997. *Inquiry Strategies for Science and Mathematics Learning, It's Just Good Teach-
    ing.* Portland, OR: Northwest Regional Educational Laboratories.

National Research Council. 2000. *Inquiry and the National Science Education.* Washington, DC:
    National Academy Press.

National Research Council. 1996. *National Science Education Standards.* Washington, DC:
    National Academy Press.

Pearce, Charles. 1999. *Nurturing Inquiry, Real Science for the Elementary Classroom.* Portsmouth,
    NH: Heinemann.

Linking Literacy Development and Science

The Advent of No Child Left Behind (NCLB)

As schools across the nation became more and more pressured to meet the proficiency standards in reading and mathematics, science and social studies moved to the background and in some cases was ignored all together; however, the landscape has now changed. The testing of science is to be included in NCLB in many states and districts have once again made science instruction a priority. With this new surge in science

Voice from the Field

Implementation of the expectations of NCLB has been a significant challenge for our teachers. The competition between subjects for instructional time is daunting. When time within the school day requires 90 to 120 minutes for reading, followed by additional time for reading intervention, along with the push for math competency, science has been moved to the background in many instances. When teachers do teach science, as they are required by our district, many are compelled to have the students read science literature books and don't engage the students in district-provided hands-on kits. Nor do they know how to make the connections between the literacy books they are using and the content in science they are to develop.

—*Dr. Michael B. Cowan, Associate Superintendent,*
Mesa Unified Schools, Mesa, Arizona

requirements comes the challenge of making time within the school day. Dr. Cowan clearly points to the challenge this creates for his teachers as well as the effect it has on how science is taught. Will science be taught for meaning and understanding or just for the words with which to answer the test? The jury is still out and only time will tell. Help with the time issue will provide teachers with the strategies and techniques to those vital science-literacy connections.

Finding the Balance: It's Not about Reading Time Versus Science Time

The challenge for science educators arises when they observe teachers using science time to read non-fiction books or just to read from a textbook without tying it directly to the development of overall science literacy. Dr. Cowan says it best, "I see several new teachers coming into the classroom with the basic skills to develop student literacy in mathematics and reading; however, it seems they do not have the same level of skills or the knowledge base for developing literacy in and through science." Highly effective elementary teachers of science understand how to use science as the core for their students to develop and apply their mathematics, reading, writing, art, and visual literacy skills. It does not have to be an either-or; the focus should be the crossroads where these skills connect to help students see the relevancy of learning them and develop an appreciation for in-depth learning.

Highly effective elementary teachers specifically provide their students with instruction that will:

- Familiarize them with the structure of expository text

- Promote content area vocabulary development

- Promote word identification skills

- Build reading fluency

- Emphasize and directly teach how, why, when, and where to use a repertoire of comprehension strategies

Effective teachers recognize that their students need to be able to read and understand content-specific vocabulary and text that characterizes science materials. This can be a struggle for many students. If they don't provide these skills, then as their students move beyond elementary school the pressure on them to understand and read expository text will continue to increase. Therefore it is not a matter of *if* they give their students these skills and strategies, but rather a matter of *how* they give their students these skills. Effective elementary teachers have found the balance. They understand that to teach these skills with hands-on science experiences is to develop in-depth learning and understanding.

In this chapter we will explore an overview of reading and writing literacy development through the platform of science, techniques effective teachers of science bring into their science lessons, the development of vocabulary or academic terms, and the use of science notebooks or science logs. The growing use and importance of science notebooks in helping students make the connections between science and writing, a more in-depth use is included in Chapter 4, Probing Children's Thinking.

I have chosen to focus on reading, writing, and visual literacy strategies and their development, not on what some call the "integration of science." Integration of science across the curriculum is done by many teachers through a thematic unit. There are teachers who use this in an effective way to link science across all curricular areas. However, in some cases integration has come to mean "if I read a relevant story then I've integrated my lesson" or "my students wrote a story about clouds" and "I'm using a cross-curriculum approach to my science instruction."

Highly effective teachers of science recognize that science content must be the core of a science lesson. This chapter is about the literacy skills and their development within the context of the science lessons.

What Does Connecting Inquiry-Based Science Experiences and Students' Literacy Development Look Like?

Seeds are scattered on a paper plate and a group of students gather around with their hand lenses to take a closer look. The teacher asks the groups to discuss their observations, with their partners before they share with the whole group. As the groups begin to share, the teacher records their observations on a word chart. They share that some seeds are big and round, while others are tiny as specks of pepper; some seeds are oval shaped and some seeds even have a rough feel. "They don't have a smell and you said we can't taste them," said some of the students. Big, round, oval, rough feeling, black, and brown are words describing the students' skills of observation, or their five senses.

"I wonder if the bigger the seed, the bigger the plant?" asked one of the students. "Do you think that is a testable question?" asked the teacher. "And what would we have to do to make it a fair test?" "We don't even know what kind of seeds these are, so how can we know what they need to grow?" volunteered one student. "Perhaps if we found that out first then we can know what they need to grow," said another. "What do most plants need to grow?" asked the teacher. "I know! They need sunlight, soil and water?" was the reply. The teacher replied with, "OK then, how about testing our question to see if small seeds grow small plants and big seeds grow bigger plant? We don't need to know what kind of seed it is because if we knew that then we would know how big or little the plant is going to be. But we do need to know something about plants. What kinds of soil will they need, where do we need to place them to grow, and how much water should we give them? How can we find this out?" The students chimed in: "We can read." "We could go on the Internet?" "We can ask the people who take care of the school yards."

This is inquiry science in action in a second-grade classroom. The students were engaged, observing, and communicating with one another and their teacher. As this lesson unfolded, the students might have read nonfiction books about plants, tested their questions, recorded and labeled their plant's growth, and made notes about their care of the plant in their science notebooks. They would be learning science words or academic vocabulary (roots, stems, seeds, soil, and sunlight) as well as descriptive words (bigger, smaller, brown, green, smooth, rough, etc.) and communicating their thinking through notes and drawings. They would begin by estimating how big they think the plant will get and would later see how close their estimating skills brought them to the real outcome. Application of math measurement skills would be used to show the height of the plants and how much water they used. This is all literacy development through science. Development and application of the grade-appropriate literacy skills will bring meaning and the relevance to learning to read, write, and communicate.

What Does Research Say about Reading and Writing Literacy Development through Science?

Inquiry-based science and reading emphasize a shared set of intellectual processes (e.g., observing, classifying, inferring, predicting, and communicating) and that the very same problem-solving processes are used "whether [students are] conducting science experiments or reading assigned science texts" (Padilla, Muth, and Padilla 1991). Highly skilled teachers of science recognize certain bases of cognitive development research that support their actions:

1) Learners Construct Knowledge for Themselves.

When the student encounters an experience they begin to put meaning and their own words to the experience. If students are doing an activity that involves magnets in first or second grade, they will say that the magnets "push away" from each other when you try to put the North and North or the South and South together, and when they put North and South together, they will "stick." The "push away" and the "stick" are part of their experiences, and these words need to be put upon a word wall. As the formal academic vocabulary is introduced the words "repel" and "attract" can be added. Students then begin to "construct" the knowledge for themselves. Without experiences in science, the actual "doing of science," students have nothing to tag meaning onto and the words we give them are merely what I call "empty vocabulary." These empty words, without any constructed meaning, become a laundry list for students to learn for the test. Some teachers have said to me that constructed meaning allows students to "own the word." The word is theirs and now has meaning.

2) When Students Experience a Phenomenon, They Begin to See Relationships to Their Prior Learning or Experiences.

As students experience a new phenomenon from the real world using their five senses, or "windows to the brain" as it is sometimes called (Glynn and Muth 1994), these ideas may go directly to their short-term memory to be forgotten immediately. Or these ideas may go to their working or long-term memory, the place in the brain where all the higher-order thinking skills come into play (analyzing and synthesizing, etc.) in search of other experiences on which to build. An example would be when students encounter magnets for the first time and see very quickly how the magnets will "push and pull" apart and what they "stick" to and what they do not. With this experience they begin to recognize (analyze) and recall where they have had previous experiences with magnets before. They have seen a magnet on the refrigerator door in their home. This experience or encounter with magnets will become the foundation for them to learn that certain materials "attract" magnets and certain material "repel" magnets. Thereby they begin not only to construct their own meaning but now they begin to understand relationships.

3) To Know and to Begin to See Relationships, They Need to Have Had Some Prior Knowledge.

As the students begin to try and make sense of their new concrete experiences, their brains go into their bank of prior experience, or long-term memory, to make a comparison. This process is interactive. Once students have a concrete experience that engages their five senses, they will enlarge their understanding of the experience. They need to synthesize this experience. Applying meaning to their experience depends a lot on their prior experiences. If students do not encounter magnets in the primary grades, in fourth or fifth grade when they study electricity and are asked to construct an electro-magnet or they only read about electro-magnets, they have no foundation on which to build their understanding. This is why it is critical for students to have these early experiences in the primary grades in order to build their knowledge and word bank.

Donovan and Bransford (2005) in *How Students Learn: Science in the Classroom* explain it is the total learning experience that will enhance and develop the students' literacy skills. For as students' build on their prior knowledge, develop their factual knowledge, and learn to organize this new knowledge for retrieval and application, there is an interactive relationship that provides the vital linkage of science and literacy development.

Many strategies and applications can be used to develop and apply literacy skills. Some of these are: using of science notebooks; applying content-area reading skills to decode and comprehend nonfiction text; understanding and learning to read charts, graphs and diagrams; effectively using visual/verbal literacy to help establish meaning; and being able to access relevant information through different forms of resources and technology. For the purpose of this chapter no attempt will be made to cover all of these in the depth but rather to frame the conversation in a way which will help us recognize these can be used to enhance the learning of science and give all students the tools they need to be a truly literate individual.

A Repertoire of Strategies for Incorporating Literacy Development in Science

The following organizational chart of strategies and techniques for literacy development uses the 5-E instructional model, which was introduced in Chapter 2. While these strategies are not described in great detail here, I will offer a broad range of suggestions and strategies for others to explore. In many cases strategies in stages overlap. However, it is helpful to see the stages described in order to get a sense of flow form one stage to the next.

Reading and Writing Literacy Development Strategies Framed Around the 5-E Instructional Model

Figure 3–1

5-E	Key Reading/Vocabulary Development and Writing Points

Engage

For students to be successful learners of new information they need to reflect on what they already know. When readers activate and use prior knowledge, they make the necessary connections between what they know and new information.

- *Accessing prior knowledge:*
  Strategies that will help identify students' misconceptions and their beliefs about the topic. Access prior knowledge through science talk by:

  - Discussing ideas and experiences about the students' experiences with the concept they are going to explore, i.e., "Where have you seem magnets before? Why do you think they stick to things? Do all things stick to the magnet? What might they be made of?"
  - Encouraging the students to listen to what others are saying and ask questions of other students about their experiences.
  - Listing ideas about the upcoming topic and/or the ideas and experiences students have had. This will be helpful as the students reflect upon their learning of the concept and will help them visually see where their misconceptions were occurring.

- *Visual literacy:*

  - Previewing a passage, looking at a picture
  - Constructing a graphic organizer or concept map
  - K-W-L chart

Reading strategies:

- Think-aloud with a partner to increase their understanding of the steps involved in the activity.

- Check for understanding of vocabulary in the activity or investigation guide, if one is used. This can be done by having the students read, pair-sharing before they begin.

- Reflective questioning upon completion of the investigation to build understanding and check for misconceptions.

- Brainstorming, clustering, and K-W-L charts to help with class discussion and reflection of the outcomes of their groups' investigation.

- Because if–then statements are used to form a hypothesis it is essential to explain this sequence for English Language Learners (ELLs), and for that matter all students. This can be done through modeling and writing examples.

Writing strategies:

- Writing, illustrating, and labeling in learning logs or science notebooks allows students to construct their own explanations for things they observe). This will also show the teacher quickly what students know and don't know. This type of note taking and reflective writing will help students practice their meta-cognitive skills of monitoring one's own learning and progress through the development of the concept.

Vocabulary development:

- Teachers collect a list of the students' own words they are using to describe their observations and findings. These can be placed on a word wall and/or the beginning of a concept map. This is a helpful technique for all students, but especially useful for ELLs.

continued

Figure 3–1

5-E	Key Reading/Vocabulary Development and Writing Points

Explain

Read to Learn

Without an understanding of text structure, students often have difficulty getting meaning from their content-area reading materials. Most students benefit from explicit instruction that helps them to understand and use the text structures as they encounter them in their reading materials.

Some of these strategies are:

- *Identifying special text features*: headings, subheadings, previews, summaries, photographs and illustrations, and the captions that accompany them.

- *Finding the main idea within the reading passage*: Make evident to students the relationships between the science concept and main ideas and supporting details.

- *Vocabulary development*: This is crucial for students because learners have no existing schema, or mental framework, to help them grasp the meaning of new terms and phrases. This is especially true for ELLs. Students need to develop their academic vocabulary for insuring success in science.

  - As new words are introduced in this section, instruction will unfold, giving students opportunities to construct meanings and conceptually relate them to the material they will be studying.
  - Use contextual analysis activities to help students see if they can determine the meaning of a word by the context in which it is used.
  - Provide opportunities for students as they learn the academic vocabulary to discover cognates, find root words, and use the text to discover meaning.
  - Use concept definition maps and Word Walls are strategies, which can become living vocabulary documents.
  - Have students make their own vocabulary charts for future reference.
  - Connect new vocabulary to something the students already know to help them visualize the meaning.
    "Have you ever looked through a pair of glasses? The lens in the glasses makes things bigger and this is the same thing a microscope does. It helps make small things look bigger."
  - Connect the visual to the new term. These visual symbols support the construction of a language network and logical processing of the new term.

- *Connecting content*: Develop content in conjunction with students' real-world experiences helps students relate and see the value of learning science. Some science textbooks or nonfiction books do this well, but if it is not overt then the teacher needs to help students to see these connections in order to make the new information meaningful. For instance, "Have you ever felt the sun's warmth upon your skin when you walked outside? This warmth is caused by the sun's rays hitting your skin."

- *Outlining*: Have the students read short chunks of information to develop their outlining skills in order for them to have something to reflect upon.

- *Visual literacy*: Incorporate the use of the visual/verbal connections to help the students who are emerging readers and/or second language learners see the relationship between the text and the visual.

  - Even though most of us believe we may be strongly "kinesthetic" or "auditory" or "visual," each of us take in more information visually than through all other modalities.
  - Visual tools such as pictures, charts, graphs, and diagrams help students to process and make sense out of abstract information.

continued

Figure 3–1

5-E	Key Reading/Vocabulary Development and Writing Points

Explain
continued

■ *Organizational patterns:* Teachers can help students find how the ideas and information are arranged in the text. Once this is accomplished the student will recognize the pattern and learn how to read and process the information.

■ *Compare/contrast:* Reporting similarities and differences between or among two or more things will help students look for signal words when items are being compared.

■ *Think-aloud:* This provides opportunities to help the students look at the titles, subtitles, graphics, and pictures to get the overall view of what the content on the pages represents. It can also be used by having two students work together before or after they have read the information to connect information to their prior knowledge, verbalize what is happening, and help with understanding of what has been read.

■ *Reading pairs:* These can be used to help students who are struggling with reading at grade level or who are second language learners.

■ *Concept definition:* This is reporting characteristics common to a concept. It requires the learner to demonstrate their understanding of term's meaning in relation to similar terms. Using concept definition maps for particular concepts at the beginning of a unit will activate students' prior knowledge. As students learn more about these concepts during the unit and develop a deeper understanding, they revisit the map and add to or change things. This then becomes a work in progress, a living vocabulary document.

■ *Reflective writing:* Writing will help students explain relationships among ideas and make connections between their explore activity, their past experiences, and their new learning about the science concept.

Extend

■ Application problem of the concept being developed both through activities and writing.

■ *Engage the students in a debate*: Have them examine two sides of an issue. For example, when learning about predator–prey relationships, should wolves be allowed to run free in Yellowstone Park?

■ *Team report:* Have students interview someone in the field they are studying—an example would be the school electrician if studying electricity.

■ *Writing and analyzing fiction:* Writing stories that incorporate the new science concepts in a creative way. This will help students synthesize their learning.

■ *Construct a discussion web to help students see both sides of an issue:* This will give all the students opportunities to assume responsibility and share their own ideas in discussion. These can be used not only to engage in an issue but also to give them time to think about their own views and then share these with a partner.

Evaluate

■ Answering questions and/or writing a summary of their learning and reflections in their science notebooks.

■ Designing an investigation to demonstrate understanding of the concept. This can be either written or actually designed.

■ Writing about a situation or problem you need to solve.

■ Completing and sharing a graphic organizer of either the vocabulary of concept(s) which where developed.

■ Using a Venn diagram

■ Comparison essay requiring students to compare and contrast the similarities and differences between two categories of things.

Using Science-Related Fiction and Fiction Trade Books to Promote Science Literacy

There are many different ways of using trade books to make connections with the learning of science concepts. Exceptional teachers use children's literature to help motivate and captivate their students' interest, to get the students engaged and ready to learn a new concept, and as a way to help make students feel comfortable with the information they are learning within real settings. Well-chosen literature reinforces the idea that science is a part of the lives of ordinary people, people who have a love of science and learning about the world around them and who want to share their sense of wonder. When scientists with diverse backgrounds are depicted working in science laboratories or out in the field, this can help bridge multicultural and equity connections. Finding literature that helps dispel gender roles is equally important. Many books help students see science heroes, such as the naturalist Jean Craighead George and Astronaut Sally Ride, as role models who took their love of science and made it a rewarding career.

Effective elementary teachers will have a wide variety of books within their classrooms and probably in their personal library. Many have shared some of their criteria they use for judging these books.

What is the Content of the Book?

- Is the coverage appropriate for the purpose?
- Is the material within the comprehension and interest range of my students?
- Is there a balance of factual and connectional material?
- Does the story encourage curiosity and further inquiry?
- Does the story connect to the curriculum content or standards I am covering?
- Are the facts and concepts presented accurately and realistically?
- Is the information presented up-to-date? (Space, dinosaurs, earth changes, solar system, biology, etc. need constant updating.)
- Are facts and fantasy distinguished?
- Is the content up to date?

How Are the Illustrations or Photographs Used as Part of the Story?

- Do the illustrations or photographs provide clues to promote students' understanding of the content?
- Are the illustrations authentic, accurate, and consistent with the text?
- Do the illustrations promote gender equity and cultural diversity?
- Will the illustrations help set the mood of the book?

There are many websites devoted to helping teachers find and use quality children's literature. An excellent source for science books is *Search It! Science*, which can be found at http://searchit.heinemann.com. This site has more than 4,200 titles and is regularly updated. It is designed for teachers and students. Many professional organizations, such as American Association for the Advancement of Science (AAAS) and National Science Teachers Association (NSTA), review and list their recommended science trade books annually. The lists are endless and they can be a challenge for teachers to use these resources not in place of active science learning, but to enhance active learning by develop meaningful science literacy for their students.

VOICE FROM THE FIELD

Science makes the world come alive for students. The skills that are learned in science cut across the curriculum. They learn to ask questions, set up investigations, how to read, write, and record information. It is where everything comes together for them. And for some of our students, who may not be the ones who love it naturally or have that natural ability, it will help them see the relevance of learning science. Then perhaps when they go into middle and high school they will be successful.

—*Principal Michael Hallock, Spectrum Elementary School, Gilbert Public Schools, Gilbert, Arizona, on his philosophy of science and literacy connections*

The Payoff for Linking Literacy Development and Science

With the blockage of time given for different classroom subjects in this era of NCLB, teachers have segregated learning into separate "pods." This segregation has made it much more difficult for the classroom teacher to plan in more of a cross-disciplinary way that will flow naturally as their day progresses. It takes time for planning, and a highly skilled teacher of science can mentor novice teachers in making vital connections. Most teachers were never shown how to do this in their pre-service classes. And as teachers are being bombarded with more accountability, and given the growing number of ELLs in our classrooms, the payoff for the time spent to develop these connections and practice using these applications will be not only the time savings for the teacher, but increasing students' language fluency.

Reading and writing literacy development and science cannot and should not be separated. Learning strategies to read expository text tied to meaningful science experiences will help our students to be successful in middle school and beyond.

References

Douglas, Rowena, M. Klentschy, K. Worth, and W. Binder. 2006. *Linking Science & Literacy in the K–8 Classroom.* Arlington, VA: NSTA Press.

Hill, Jane, and K. Flynn. 2006. *Classroom Instruction that Works with English Language Learners.* Alexandria, VA: Association for Supervision and Curriculum Development.

Lowery, Larry. 1998. "How the New Science Curriculums Reflect Brain Research." *Education Leadership* (Nov. pgs. 26–28) Alexandria, VA: Association for Curriculum and Supervision.

Glynn, S., and D. Muth. 1994. "Reading and Writing to Learn Science: Achieving Scientific Literacy." *Journal of Research in Science Teaching* 31 (9): 1057–73.

Marzano, Robert, D. Pickering, and J. Pollock. 2000. *Classroom Instruction that Works: Research-Based Strategies for Increasing Student Achievement.* Alexandria, VA: Association for Supervision and Curriculum Development.

Saul, Wendy. 2002. Science *Workshop: Reading, Writing, and Thinking Like a Scientist*, Second Edition. Portsmouth, NH: Heinemann.

Search It! Science http://searchit.heinemann.com

CHAPTER 4

Probing Children's Thinking

"I thought I taught it, I know I taught it, and then I figured out that half of them just didn't get it. I just had to find a tool for seeing inside my students' heads."

—*Stacey Green, fourth-grade teacher, Hopi Elementary School, Scottsdale, Arizona*

The Difference between Knowing and "Knowing"

Since Socrates first started asking questions, probing students' thinking to find out what they know has been part of teaching and learning. Today the impact of achievement scores drives decisions that are made about learners' progress. Who will react to these decisions? What information will be helpful?

In this era of high stakes testing it is very difficult for teachers to find the time to translate individual knowledge of a student's progress into designing a path for each individual to take in order to help them master the concept in question. There are many avenues that can be incorporated into the learning process to help inform and illuminate the path the teacher must take to insure all children have the opportunity to learn. Effective teachers have practiced and honed their skills by using several techniques. They can, and do, find ways to uncover their students' thinking.

Highly skilled teachers wants—and needs—to know who is making progress; however, they also want to know what comes next in the learning process. They want continuous information and feedback about each student's journey to each standard or benchmark. They know that information needs is for the student, the administration, parents, and the government. They understand that the purpose of assessment is to encourage learning. Students must master the content and take responsibility for their own learning. But a highly effective teacher employs assessment *for* learning rather than using an assessment *of* learning.

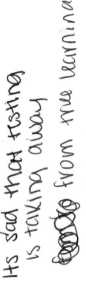

Its sad that testing is taking away from true learning

37

Assessments *for* learning are employed by teachers to help students believe in themselves, help them understand the results, and figure out what to do next. They realize that they might not have understood it the first time it was presented but it is OK and to choose to keep trying. Assessments *for* learning inform the teacher about the difference between a student just knowing the answer for the assessment benchmark (the OF learning), and "knowing," as in having internalized the concept in a way that is meaningful and will lay a firm foundation for future learning.

Highly effective elementary teachers use many strategies for probing and uncovering their students' thinking and understanding of science. Rather than focusing on just assessment in this chapter, we will examine some of the many strategies effective teachers of elementary science use to encourage students' "knowing" the science concepts.

Children's Minds Are Not Blank Slates!

A classroom science table is covered with a variety of crisp, colored leaves as well as some that are green. The teacher, Rae Unkovich, had collected them from the schoolyard. Mrs. Unkovich, an experienced and skilled teacher, knows that having her students observe is an effective way to begin a science lesson. As her students stand around the table, Mrs. Unkovich asks, "What do you notice about these leaves?" Different students respond by talking about how they are different colors, as in "some are brown, some are yellow, some are in-between with some green on them, and some are totally green." As the students go through their observations, Mrs. Unkovich asks, "Why do you think some of the leaves are different colors and some are still green?" Juan says, "It's getting cold and all the green comes out of them." "Perhaps the sun turned them that way," says Jamie. "I believe it has to do with insects or something that is sucking out all the green," replies Tamera. "I know," says Kelly, "The sap ran right out of them because they got too hot and then they sweated just like we do."

Mrs. Unkovich's students clearly demonstrate that children have many different beliefs and ideas about the natural world they see around them. Some thought that leaves change color due to the changing of the weather, others thought that insects or "bugs" suck out the color, and one held the notion that leaves "sweat" like people do. Children enter school already having substantial knowledge of the natural world, much of it implicit. They may not have the right or scientific explanation about a natural phenomenon; however, they do have their own way of thinking and making sense about the world around them. Uncovering and discovering each child's system of reasoning and thinking is very important in the learning process. As it was once thought that young children were just concrete and simplistic thinkers, the research evidence now shows that their thinking is surprisingly sophisticated (Duschl, Schweingruber, and Shouse 2006).

I try to find different ways to engage my students when I'm beginning a new lesson. Their comments about the leaves told me they had already tried to form answers about the colored leaves they see this time of year. As part of our third-grade curriculum we study the seasons. I try to start it at this time of year because the students are aware of the days growing cooler and the leaves beginning to change and drop off the trees. This is something my students notice and think of as an indicator of the season. We will cover animal and plant changes in our fall unit, in which the students will learn a simple explanation of why some trees leaves change colors and fall off and others stay green.

If I had just jumped right into talking about fall and showing the leaves as one of the indicators we see around us, then I would have never known some of their ideas. One of the techniques I use when listening to their thinking is to record their comments on a chart. I do not tell them if their thinking is right or wrong, but as we learn about the concept I'll refer back to the chart and as a group we mark out which are not correct ideas. This is a little different from the K-W-L charts, which I use as well. I'm also careful not to put names by the comments because by the time we get into the fun of learning science they forget who said what.

—*Rae Unkovich, third-grade teacher, Edu-Prize Charter Elementary School, Gilbert, Arizona*

Children will also hold on to their thinking and misconceptions even when they have gone through a series of experiences proving otherwise. It is surprising to note that unless the teacher is persistent in uncovering students' thinking, and getting at their misconceptions, even when they put the answer down that the teacher might want, they'll just walk away in the end believing they are still are right. The following is a wonderful example of this.

Engagement through Elicitation is Key to Beginning Scientific Inquiry

"Elicitation gives students the opportunity to make their ideas and reasons explicit as they begin the study of a unit topic. It engages them and also alerts them to what they will be thinking and learning about in the upcoming instruction" (Keeley, Eberle, and Farrin 2005, 2). Many elementary teachers today who are not comfortable teaching science con- tent, and who are even more uncomfortable with children's questions about science will, more often than not, jump right into a lesson. They feel that by asking the one or two questions given at the beginning of the science textbook and/or lesson guide that they have done enough to engage students. Highly effective teachers of science engage through elicitation of thinking. They are aware their students have their own understanding of the natural world and are anxious to find out what these students are thinking.

"Students enter the study of science with a vast array of such preconceptions based on their everyday experiences. Teachers will need to engage those ideas if students are to understand science" (Donovan and Bransford 2005, 399). Therefore, if their initial understanding is not engaged, they may fail to grasp the new concepts and information, or they may learn them for purposes of a test but revert to their preconceptions outside the classroom (Brandsford, Brown, and Cocking 2000). The major instructional recommendations presented by *How People Learn* are embodied, to a great extent, in three fundamental principles of learning, of which understanding that students are not a blank slate and do have preconceptions is the first.

Children often interpret phenomena from a "common sense" point of view that can lead to misconceptions. Thinking the "green in the leaf was gone because the leaf was able to sweat," made perfect sense to Kelly. She didn't have any other explanation and therefore she made one up. Far too often children who have these ideas, or alternate frameworks, about the natural world will continue to hold on to this thinking. Therefore, effective teaching involves changing beliefs that knowledge is passed on from teacher to student, to recognizing the need to engage students in rethinking their ideas, which results in increased learning (Keeley 2005).

Before and during the Science Lesson: Using Science Probes to Get at Student Thinking

There is a wide range of summative assessment and instructional material available to teachers. However, very few ready-made science formative assessments are available that can enhance and support teachers' pedagogical content knowledge. Senior Science Program Director of the Maine Mathematics and Science Alliance (MMSA) Page Keeley and her colleagues have researched, developed, and field tested a series of formative assessment, probes, that help teachers uncover students' thinking. These have been designed to be used by any teacher in any instructional context. These probes have been developed for diagnostic and monitoring purposes as they are assessments of learning. They are meant to reveal the types of misconceptions students have about common science concepts. Page Keeley explains:

> The probes are designed to provide quick and targeted feedback on students' ideas and of learning. As teachers read the students' explanations, they will notice similar ideas held by a number of students as well as idiosyncratic ones help by individual students. Overall, they are meant to be quick and easy for all teachers to use to help inform adjustments to curriculum and instruction in order to improve their students' learning.

The assessment probes are designed to find out what students think about particular foundational concepts identified in the National Science Education Standards and the AAAS Benchmark as well as cognitive research literature. In many cases there is no one "right" answer, but an attempt to reveal the students' thinking about the ideas and provide insight to the teacher as to next steps for instruction. The assessment probes provided by the book *Uncovering Students Ideas in Science* (Keeley, Eberle, and Farrin 2006), provide information about:

- How students' ideas may differ from one grade level to the next

- How ready individual students are for instruction

- Ideas students have before instruction

- Whether conceptual change is occurring

- Whether students retain the accepted scientific ideas years after instruction or revert back to their prior knowledge

- Gaps that exist in a school's or district's curriculum

A Sample Probe: Cookie Crumbles

The purpose of this assessment probe is to elicit students' ideas about conservation of matter using ordinary objects such as a cookie. The probe is specifically designed to find out whether students believe there will be a change in weight when a whole object is broken up into many small pieces (Keeley, Eberle, and Farrin 2006, 61–65).

As you look over these authentic classroom samples from second grade you come to realize how telling they are about the students' thinking. The correct answer is C—the weight would be the same. The total weight of the parts, in this case the cookie crumbs, is equal to the weight of the unbroken cookie. The only thing that changed was the shape or arrangement of the cookie; no new matter was added or taken away. Conservation of matter is a physical principle that applies to the ordinary changes in objects as well as the physical and chemical changes in substances. In both cases, matter cannot be created nor destroyed in an ordinary or chemical change.

The ideas of conservation and change of objects are developed in the upper elementary grades. Knowing the sum of the parts of an object is the same as the whole object is a grade-level expectation in the National Science Education Standards. As you look at these three examples you can clearly see which two children had the same thinking; that because the cookie was bigger than the crumbs it would weigh more. It is here an effective teacher of science will design some hands-on investigations for these students to help change their misconception and establish their thinking. If the teacher does not take the time to probe

Figure 4–1

Cookie Crumbles

Imagine you have a whole cookie. You break the cookie into tiny pieces and crumbs. You weigh all of the pieces and crumbs. How do you think the weight of the whole cookie compares to the total weight of all the cookie crumbs? Circle the best answer.

A The whole cookie weighs more than all of the cookie crumbs.

B All of the cookie crumbs weigh more than the whole cookie.

C The whole cookie and all of the cookie crumbs weigh the same.

Describe your thinking. Provide an explanation for your answer.

I think C is the coreckt anser because you have 1 cookie and if you way it before you brak it it will way somthing and it will It will waye the same it will just be broken.

Figure 4–2

Cookie Crumbles

Imagine you have a whole cookie. You break the cookie into tiny pieces and crumbs. You weigh all of the pieces and crumbs. How do you think the weight of the whole cookie compares to the total weight of all the cookie crumbs? Circle the best answer.

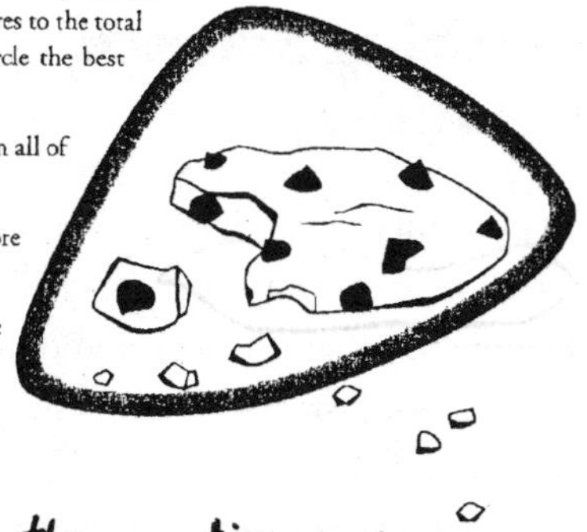

A The whole cookie weighs more than all of the cookie crumbs.

B All of the cookie crumbs weigh more than the whole cookie.

C The whole cookie and all of the cookie crumbs weigh the same.

Describe your thinking. Provide an explanation for your answer.

I think A becoase the cookie crumbs and pieces are smaller and the whole cookie is bigger and the whole cookie would weigh more because its bigger.

Figure 4–3

Cookie Crumbles

Imagine you have a whole cookie. You break the cookie into tiny pieces and crumbs. You weigh all of the pieces and crumbs. How do you think the weight of the whole cookie compares to the total weight of all the cookie crumbs? Circle the best answer.

A The whole cookie weighs more than all of the cookie crumbs.

B All of the cookie crumbs weigh more than the whole cookie.

C The whole cookie and all of the cookie crumbs weigh the same.

Describe your thinking. Provide an explanation for your answer.

I Pick A Becuse. cookies are biger then crumbs and then Big cookies. crumbs are smaller.

the students' thinking at the beginning, students' are likely to retain their preconceptions, regardless of the foundation being laid for them by the teacher. Then as the student moves on to middle school, where they will be ready to use conservation reasoning to explain changes in substances, they will still hold on to their original explanations.

OK, I'm Teaching Science, but How Do I Know They Are Learning?

In today's classroom atmosphere of high-stakes standardized testing, teachers are constantly looking for evidence of learning. The challenge for teachers becomes the scarcity of time or taking the time to actually discover and uncover what their students are thinking, and to see that they are not just putting an answer down at the end-of-chapter test to satisfy the requirement that they have learned what was presented to them or what they have read. How then can we make reasonable decisions about what counts as science learning? What are the expectations for performance that show evidence of student thinking?

When you walk into a classroom and hear the teacher asking only "how, what, and why" questions, you might assume right away these are more in the level of interrogation questions. Often children feel badly because they do not know the right answer. For

First use
Describe (lets take a
then why a closer look)

example, "Why does a ball fall to the ground when you throw it up?" might prompt the student to answer, "Because of gravity," when in fact they may have read about "gravity" and/or have heard the word, perhaps even on a vocabulary list given prior to the lesson, but when asked to explain the word they will have no idea what it is. A highly effective teacher may have begun with, "Describe what happens when you toss a ball into the air?" This question will stimulate thinking. It says "take a closer look"; it is an invitation to learn. The right question asks children to show rather than to say the answer. These are referred to as "productive" questions, because they stimulate productive activity.

In an inquiry-oriented lesson, an effective teacher will know when and how to ask the right question at the right time in the sequence of the students' learning. This is not an easy task and not something a novice teacher will become acquainted with in their science methods classes. It requires professional development and mentoring to establish questioning styles; however, they become very powerful tools and extremely useful for teachers when they are in those "think on their feet" situations. It helps them to respond to and listen to what the children are saying and begin to move their teaching from that of imparting factual knowledge to promoting the true meaning of scientific inquiry—a way of thinking and finding out about the world around them.

When Mrs. Unkovich asked, "Why do you think some of the leaves have turned colors and some are still green?" this could have been a situation where some children would be afraid they were going to give the right or wrong answer. However, since these children were accustomed to being able to freely say what they were thinking without feeling someone would say "That's not right," it was apparent to the observer the teacher had established the atmosphere of trust. In some cases the "What do you think?" or the "Why do you think?" might come premature in the lesson. In this situation, the question was meant to be an attention-focusing question.

Wynn Harlen, noted researcher and author in science education, has written extensively about the value of asking productive questions. She describes wrong questions as questions that tend to begin with such innocent interrogatives as *why*, *how*, or *what* (Harlen 2001). These are not necessarily bad beginnings for questions, because productive questions can begin with these words; the difference is if the students have actually had an experience, they can know for themselves. The distinction between *productive* and *unproductive* questions is whether or not they promote children's activity and reasoning (Elstgeest in Harlen 2001: 34).

Elstgeest offers the following suggestions for productive questions:

Asking "Productive" Questions

1. Study the effect on students of asking different kinds of questions so that you can distinguish the *productive* from the *unproductive*.

2. Use the simplest form of attention-focusing question during initial exploration to help students take note of details that they might otherwise overlook.

3. Use measuring and counting questions to nudge students from purely qualitative observations towards quantitative observation.

4. Use comparison questions to help children order their observations and data.

5. Use action questions to encourage experimentation and the investigation of relationships.

6. Use problem-posing questions when students are capable of setting up for themselves hypotheses and situations to test them.

7. Choose the type of question to suit the children's experience in relation to the particular subject of inquiry.

Suggestions for "Why" and "How" Questions

1. When asking questions to stimulate student' reasoning, make sure they include "What do you think about . . ." or "Why do you think . . ."

2. Don't ask questions of this type until students have had the necessary experience they need so that they can reason from evidence.

3. When students ask "why" questions, consider whether they have the experience to understand the answer.

4. Don't be afraid to say you don't know an answer, or that no one knows (if it is a philosophical question).

5. Break up questions whose answers would be too complex into ones that concern relationships the children can find out about and understand.

6. Take children's questions seriously, as an expression of what interests them, even if the questions cannot be answered, don't discourage the asking.

questions are scaffolded too

Productive questions are the ones that are needed to promote scientific inquiry. These questions will help children answer questions from firsthand experiences instead of just reading about it or being told. The difference between effective teachers and those who are not as effective is very clear if you listen to their questioning strategies, and how they scaffold them; simply using higher cognitive questions does not guarantee high-level responses. It is much more effective if teachers use a wide array of questioning to increase all their students thinking and responses.

Rae Unkovich explained to me that it took her a long time to learn how to question, and one of the ways she used to get better at asking questions was to look at the science textbook and see if the questions used in the lesson were of the productive or unproductive type. She said this helped her to think about how she was framing her own questions. Rae is an excellent example of a highly effective teacher of science who has been willing to work at the art of teaching. She says, "It is very difficult to think on your feet when you're in the middle of a lesson about how to frame the questions to get to the direction you want the students to go; however, I've found over the years just being aware of the different kinds of question I need to ask, attention and focusing, measuring, comparison, action, and problem-posing, etc., has certainly helped me become a better all-around teacher in all the subjects."

The Use of Wait Time for Encouraging Children's Thinking

The concept of "wait time" as an instructional variable was invented by Mary Budd Rowe (1972). She found in her research that the periods of wait time rarely lasted more than 1.5 seconds in typical classrooms. She discovered, however, that when these periods of silence lasted at least 3 seconds, many positive things happened to students' and teachers' behaviors and attitudes (Rowe 1987).

When students are given more time to formulate their responses, they are likely to participate more in a classroom discussion and the length and correctness of their responses increase. Wait time is valuable for all students, but particularly valuable for ELLs because it allows them time to think about not only what they are going to say, but also how they are going to say it in English (Hill and Flynn 2006).

Some researchers are now calling "wait time" "think time" (Stahl 1990). However it is referred to, most science educators call it wait time, and the technique is the same. It is a period of uninterrupted silence by the teacher. Teachers will often speak of two kinds of wait time. "Wait time 1" refers to the amount of time they allow to elapse after posing a question and *before* a student begins to speak. "Wait time 2" refers to the amount of time a teacher waits *after* a student has stopped speaking before saying anything. By simply increasing the wait time from 3 to 7 seconds, teachers say it will usually result in an increase in:

1. Length of student responses

2. Number of unsolicited responses

3. Frequency of student questions,

4. Number of responses from less capable children or ELLs

5. Student-to-student interactions

6. Incidence of speculative responses.

When teachers pause after a student's response to a question (wait time 2), and when teachers do not affirm answers immediately, they find students may come up with longer, more thoughtful explanations.

Teachers of elementary science have said they believe there is a direct correlation between their wait time, increased student achievement, and increased student participation in inquiry. There is some research that does affirm this. Tobin and Stahl both have shown that when teachers increase their wait time to more than three seconds in class discussions, achievement on higher-cognitive-level science test items increases significantly. This holds for test items involving content, process skills, and items involving probabilistic reasoning.

Wait time ensures that students will have time to think, reflect, and participate in the discussion. There are always those children who want to be the first and/or always shout out the answer. By using wait time children begin to understand they need to think before they respond. However, care must be taken in applying wait time judiciously. The optimal wait time for a given question should be adjusted to the cognitive level of the question, and student's responses should be carefully monitored.

Bringing Wonder into the Classroom

In the classroom of a highly effective teacher of science students are stimulated immediately by their surroundings. Displays and collections of items such as shells, leaves, rock-sand in one classroom I visited there was a display of different kinds of birds' feet on loan from the state game and wildlife department. What a great invitation to stimulate children to begin to think and wonder! These collections evoke curiosity. Each display had questions to probe children's curiosity. "Describe how the nails are shaped on the foot of the bird. Do some look like they might be good for living in trees? Are there any ways you could tell this by your observations?" Just putting out a collection is OK, but putting out a collection and ask questions to spark curiosity is so much better.

In these classrooms you will probably also see a science corner where the children go and investigate using materials independently, or a "question of the week" to stimulate their thinking about what they are going to be learning in science. It might be an extension investigation for reinforcement of a concept. There are usually bulletin boards that engage, and provide a place to write questions (perhaps on a wipe-off board). I've observed teachers who allow students to write the question and have different groups find the answer through reading, researching on the Internet, or asking an authority. Then the groups will post their answers. What a wonderful way for all the students to become engaged! Exploring atmospheres provide opportunities for children to see science as a way of thinking about the world around them and asking questions about this natural world. Science makes the classroom come alive!

Science text materials and teacher guides provide questions for the teacher to use to stimulate their student's thinking, but often they don't offer much help in the way of what to do to stimulate the *students* to ask questions. Many teachers are very wary of having their students ask too many questions. They fear not knowing the answer, or the question might not even be answerable within their scope of understanding, or it is a testable question that might be beyond the capabilities of the materials in their classroom.

"Is God Bigger Than the Clouds?" (and Other Unanswerable Questions)

Wynne Harlen's book *Primary Science, Taking the Plunge* provides some excellent examples of how to handle students' spontaneous questions. For instance, take the questions, "If god made the world, then who made god?" and "Are there people in outer space?" Each of these has no known answer; therefore, it is one that the child is wondering about. Each of these might be deferred by saying "We really do not know," or "It is beyond my scope of understanding." Another example of a spontaneous question, "What makes it rain?" is, however, something the teacher could help the child to understand through a simple water cycle investigation. The second question is one that is testable and could be explained to the child. Therefore the teacher could set this up by responding with the strategy "Let's see what we can do to understand more" (Harlen 2001, 43–44).

Helping Students Change "Why" Questions into "How" Questions to Make Testable Questions

Elementary teachers, most of whom do not have an extensive science background, might even feel frightened by the child's questions. Some say, "I've tried the 'let's find out together' approach, and it is very hard to do." Many teachers will identify with these remarks, but a highly effective teacher would recommend taking the children's questions and making them more practical. In other words, they would change them into questions that can be tested, researched, or to you which one can apply an action-oriented approach, as in "Let's see what we can do to understand more?". Harlen describes this as the teaching skill of being able to "turn" the question (Harlen 2001, 44).

You have walked into a classroom where the students have been reading and discussing a story about polar bears from their literature book. One child asks, "How long do polar bears live?" Another asks, "If they eat seals what else do they eat?" and still another, "If they go into the cold water, why don't they freeze to death?" and "We learned ducks have feathers and oil in their skin to help them, but polar bears have only fur!" The teacher does a quick scan of the questions to see which of these might be turned into scientific inquiry. The first two can be answered by reading or through Internet research; however, the last one, "Why don't they freeze to death?" can be investigated by having the students set up experiments that will demonstrate how things are insulated. This particular teacher did have his students look at and think about all kinds of insulations. Then they tried different insulators in cold water by wrapping their hands with the items, putting their hands into a plastic bags and then dipping the hand into a bucket of ice-cold water. After testing several different things—cotton wrapping, wool cloth, cardboard—they actually began to look at polar bears' features. Realizing they are quite large and heavy, they began to think about a protective layer of fat. They actually hit upon using lard to cover their hands. What a joyous moment that was for this teacher! Yes, he could have said, "Polar bears are insulated with their protective layer of fat." But not this effective science teacher—he saw the moment of inquiry and took his students on the journey of discovery.

This process can be summed up in the following steps:

1. Analyze the question.

2. Consider if it can be turned around into a testable one. Is the question a productive one?

3. Have the students think about how to test it.

4. Set up the investigation.

5. Communicate the results.

A teacher who models how to ask questions and encourages his or her students provides an atmosphere that invites students to learn. Inquiry-based learning need not always be a hands-on experience. The students can be engaged in inquiry through reading, research, discussions, and interviewing others. Learning how to support student learning through skillful questioning strategies requires ongoing professional development, discussion among peers, and modeling for most teachers.

Science Notebooks: A Growing Strategy for Linking Science and Writing

Science notebooks are becoming an integral component of a highly effective science program. Growing in popularity, they provide the opportunity for students to apply their writing skills and exploring their own thinking as they describe, explain, formulate, persuade, and question scientific experiences and phenomena (Douglas, Klentschy, Worth, and Binder 2006).

To view samples of science notebooks visit www.sciencenotebooks.org. This site is made possible through the North Cascades and Olympic Science Partnership whose Principal Investigator is Dr. George (Pinkey) Nelson.

....

"Scientists Write, So I Should Too?" —Robbie Beck, Second-grade Student

Science notebooks provide an opportunity for students to record and share their thinking and their learning before, during, and after a science investigation. They reflect a chronological accounting of the progression of an investigation as the student records questions, materials, procedures, observations, data, explanations, and reflections. Notebooks are silent companions that can be referred to and reread throughout the investigation. As a working document, the science notebook is a rough draft whose primary audience is the student. Using it as a paper reminder, students refer to it during science discussions, and rely on it as a source of information for expanded presentational writing opportunities such as articles and reports.

A science notebook is:

■ A student thinking tool

I've been teaching for over twenty-five years and I've always been a constructivist teacher. What I mean by this is instead of saying I'm going to show you how to do it this way and now do it, I like to give my students some leeway to develop their own thinking. When I first began using science notebooks with my class, I was very frustrated because I felt I was being very prescriptive. It just didn't feel right. Then through our MSP (Math–Science Partnerships) and NSF (National Science Foundation) grant we have here in the state of Washington, I attended a summer professional development institute which showed me a different way to use notebooking. Now I've gone the route that Brian Campbell and Lori Fulton describe in the book *Science Notebooks, Writing About Inquiry* (Campbell and Fulton 2003).

Using science notebooks was such a messy process in the beginning, and getting my students to record what they were thinking was a long process. But because I didn't prescribe what their notebooks were to look like and didn't tell them what to record as they were doing their investigations, they came to learn on their own that if they didn't write down the information and/or label the drawing, when they went back to look over it or show it to me, something was missing. I could not have taught them this valuable lesson. It just came to them because it began to make much more sense. Now that we have begun, I think as these students go through the grades they will understand the value of using notebooking."

—*Lisa Conlon, third- to fifth-grade team, Larrabee Elementary School, Bellingham School District, Bellingham, Washington*

- An organizer for inquiry question and what is learned
- A way to access and process the learning utilizing various modalities (writing, drawing, and discussion)
- A means for all students to work at their level (ELLs)
- A place for writing rough drafts based on hands-on learning
- A formative assessment tool for teachers

I learned about science notebooks at the National Science Teachers Association National Conference, in some sessions that I attended with a team from my district. The science notebook just grabbed me as a different way to have my students share their thinking and organize their data. As I began using it in my classroom, it became a two-way street. What they put down in their notebooks showed me how I was teaching-it helped me to, in a way, see inside my students' brains.

I have my students draw pictures, make graphs, write or otherwise record information from our activities. I always have an objective for my lesson that is the learning outcome. Say for instance when we were doing plants, my objective for one lesson was to have them explain, after they had a hands-on experience, through writing, or drawing why seeds absorb water, and how they change when they do so. The students had to understand that seeds absorb water to begin growth, and that their sizes change, as well as the concepts of mass and weight. If they didn't label it or write about it, then I knew they didn't get it. I did a summary after the lesson and we drew what is called a "line of learning." If they got the idea of absorption and had shown it in some way, then they could check it off. If they didn't record this, then under their line of learning they wrote about, or drew something absorbing. This way I help all my students to learn the concept. It doesn't say to some kids, "You didn't get it, therefore you're dumb." What it says is, "Under the line of learning is something you didn't quite focus on the first time around." Kids are very honest and when I collect the science notebooks it helps me see exactly who is getting the concept and who needs more help.

—*Stacey Green, Elementary Presidential Awardee and fourth-grade teacher, Hopi Elementary School, Scottsdale, Arizona*

Figure 4–4

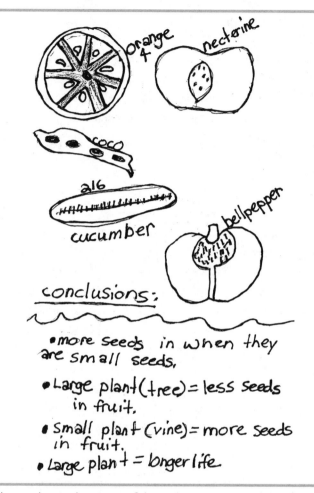

This shows the student's drawings of their observations combined with the line of learning showing their notes from the whole group discussion and summary.

Figure 4–5

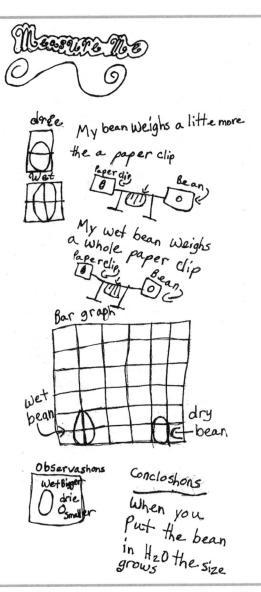

The student has combined words and diagrams to describe their scientific understanding. By allowing them the choice of how they express and record their data, the teacher can see the student's thought process and thinking.

Figure 4–6

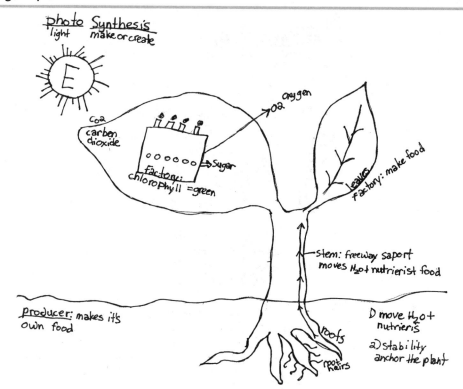

This demonstrates a student's use of pictures as a way to express and describe their understanding of a process.

Figure 4–7

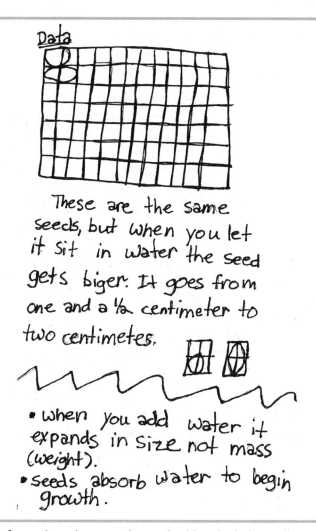

Data

These are the same seeds, but when you let it sit in water the seed gets biger. It goes from one and a ¼ centimeter to two centimetes.

• when you add water it expands in size not mass (weight).
• seeds absorb water to begin growth.

This is an example of a student choosing the method by which they will record data. They have chosen to draw the seeds, but have added graph paper to demonstrate the size difference. The line of learning has the main points I wanted them to have, but you see their conclusion mirrors these ideas directly above. This enables the teacher to see that they have the concept, and where they have misconceptions.

Figure 4–8

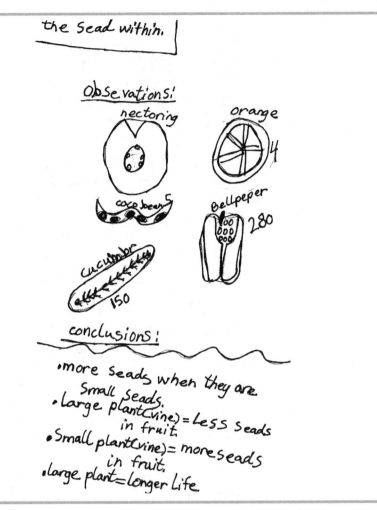

the Sead within.

Obsevations:

nectoring

orange 4

coco bean 5

Bellpeper 280

cucumber 150

conclusions!

• more seads when they are small seads.
• Large plant(vine) = Less Seads in fruit.
• Small plant(vine) = more seads in fruit.
• Large plant = longer life

This is an example of "a picture is worth a thousand words". The student has created a detailed diagram to show the differences in the seeds and pods. The line of learning shows how the student's drawing matches the conclusion.

Science notebooks and other ways of writing in science provide students with the ability to see the value of learning to write. Their science notebook entries provide opportunities for them to practice writing in the various modes—descriptive, explanatory, procedural, recounting, and persuasive—while learning the science concept. The guiding principle in determining the mode of writing is purpose. Teachers of course will still need to explicitly teach the structure and language of the modes of nonfiction writing in their language arts lessons; however, the application, reflection, and meaning making can come in the context of science.

Summary Thoughts

Assessment *for* learning creates a culture of confidence. Assessment *for* learning is how we can use assessment to help students learn more. A teacher's job is to help children believe that they are capable learners. When assessments are only *of* learning, then they are just to see if the child has met that mark, not if the child has internalized the concept. Teachers need to have clear and appropriate targets for their students, but also need to have accurate classroom assessments—ways to provide descriptive feedback—and student-involved assessments. In a classroom atmosphere where children feel secure and are able express their own ideas, teachers will find they will have access to the children's thinking.

Physician's creed: Above all, do no harm.
Educator's creed: Above all, do nothing to diminish hope.

References

Bransford, J., A. Brown, and R. Cocking. 2000. *How People Learn.* Washington, DC: National Academy Press.

Donovan, M. S., and J. Bransford. 2005. *How Students Learn Science in the Classroom.* Washington, DC: National Academy Press.

Douglas, R., M. Klentschy, K. Worth, and W. Binder. 2006. *Linking Science and Literacy in the K–8 Classroom.* Arlington, VA: National Science Teachers Association Press.

Duschel, R., H. Schweingruber, and A. Shouse, Editors. 2006. *Taking Science to School: Learning and Teaching Science in Grades K–8.* Washington, DC: National Academy Press.

Harlen, W. 2001. Primary Science, *Taking the Plunge*, Second Edition. Portsmouth, NH: Heinemann.

Keeley, P., F. Eberle, and L. Farrin. 2005. *Science Assessment Probes.* Arlington, VA: National Science Teachers Association Press.

Rowe, M. B. "Wait-time: Slowing Down May Be a Way of Speeding Up." *American Educator* (Spring 2006): 38–43.

Tobin, K. "The Role of Wait Time in Higher Cognitive Level Learning." *Review of Educational Research* 57 (Spring 1987).

CHAPTER 5

Designing and Delivering Effective Science Instruction

Knowing What to Teach and How to Teach It

Dr. Molina-Walters discussing her expectations of a highly effective elementary teacher of science; knowing what to teach (the content), knowing how to teach (the pedagogy), and having the essential background knowledge (the depth of conceptual understanding). In *How Students Learn Science,* the authors describe effective science instruction at the elementary level by saying core to teachers' decision making is the need to manage individual students' learning of both targeted scientific knowledge and the *ways* of knowing. For this to happen, teachers must have sufficient subject matter knowledge, including aspects

---

VOICE FROM THE FIELD

To be an effective teacher of science [teachers] first need to have a passion for science and then develop the skills for effective teaching; [they need] a balance between knowing what to teach and how to teach it. They also need to have essential background knowledge. In my science methods classes I hold students responsible for not only learning how to teach science but also knowing and understanding the content they are going to be teaching.

—*Dr. Molina-Walters EdD, School of Educational Innovation and Teacher Preparation, Arizona State University Polytechnic Campus*

of the culture of science that guide knowledge production, and must fully understand the nature of the learning goals. Therefore, when a student says that light "disappears" into paper but reflects off mirrors, a teacher's uncertainty about whether that claim is accurate will hamper their effective decision making or if a student claims an object is opaque and the question at hand is how light interacts with matter, the teacher needs to recognize that the word "opaque" describes the object and not light. Teachers need to have accurate subject matter knowledge combined with pedagogical content knowledge to be a truly effective practitioner (National Resource Council 2005, 467–68).

To improve the future of elementary science instruction, teachers must be held responsible for their content knowledge as well as pedagogical knowledge. Unfortunately, many elementary teachers who are presently in the classroom have not had the depth of preparation nor the professional development experiences to bring them up to the level needed to be effective teachers of science. The difference I have found between those who just teach science and those who do it effectively is the latter have gone beyond traditional training to acquire the needed content and skills. Most effective elementary teachers are part of a science "community of learners," either within their district or state, and belong to professional science organizations. They choose to participate in professional development experiences to improve their instruction and content knowledge base. Along with having the essential skills and knowledge base, teachers need to manage and execute inquiry-based instruction. They also need to be supported with effective curricula and materials if they are going to be truly effective. These are points we will explore in this chapter.

Defining Curriculum Coherence and Articulation

The National Science Education Standards (NSES) and Benchmarks for Science Literacy from the American Association for the Advancement of Science (AAAS) define the content of instruction by outlining what a student should know and be able to do. It is the district curriculum, usually guided by state science standards, that provides a roadmap of what content will be taught at which grade level, and how it will be aligned throughout the grade levels. How this content is organized, presented, and assessed is the backbone of classroom science instruction. In other words, classroom science instruction is driven, for the most part, by the curriculum map the district lays out for their teachers. An effective curriculum map is coherent, aligned, and makes sense as a whole.

A carefully designed curriculum is a roadmap to promote learning with understanding, and usually is framed around a series of lesson and unit structures. Such a structure helps teachers organize factual information around "big ideas" of science rather than

Backbone of Science Instruction

teaching facts in isolation. *How People Learn* describes the enterprise of education as moving students in the direction of more formal understanding (or greater expertise). To do this will require both a deepening of the information base and the development of a conceptual framework for that subject matter (NRC 2000, 17). To facilitate this type of learning, instruction must provide students with depth of factual information (not factoids) while at the same time connecting that information to the core ideas or big ideas of science.

What Is a Big Idea?

Jay McTighe and Grant Wiggins in their *Understanding by Design* model, use enduring understandings to reach the *big ideas* or *important understandings* of what we want the students to get inside of and retain after they've forgotten many of the details. What this does is help students to connect to a larger idea to provide a cognitive framework that facilitates a greater transfer of learning. In *How People Learn* (NRC 2000), one of the key factors that distinguishes "expert" learners from "novices" is the ability to organize or chunk their thinking around big ideas. It is these big ideas that you will find effective teachers providing for their students.

Some curricular materials will be focused around the big ideas; however, if the resources the teachers are using in their district do not do this, how can this happen? Most of the time it requires district or grade-level study groups to help flush these out. In some cases districts do provide a roadmap for their teachers along with the professional development to gain understanding.

One district that has provided a roadmap for its teachers is Virginia Beach City Public Schools in Virginia:

We developed science units of study with the goal of helping students to deepen their understanding of science. To accomplish this goal, each science unit is developed around big ideas or what McTighe and Wiggins call enduring understandings. Students, with the help of teachers, will uncover content and the facts associated with our state standards, through essential questions that get at the heart of the understanding(s). By providing our elementary teachers with this information, teachers can spend the time developing lessons that frame their teaching around the big ideas and essential questions. Activities within the units are aligned to an essential question. By providing teachers with this information, along with professional development, we have been able to move our teachers from just looking at science as a list of factual knowledge to understanding the big idea. For instance, a first grade student will learn that all animals have certain physical characteristics. Common physical characteristics were used by scientists to form groups. Understanding the physical characteristics of organisms, such as body coverings, leads in later grade levels to the understanding that animals have unique ways to protect themselves in order to survive. In previous years, students would not have gotten to this understanding. They would instead have learned isolated facts about mammals and birds.

—*Dr. Jenny Sue Flannagan, Elementary Science Coordinator, Virginia Beach City Public Schools, Virginia*

Figure 5–1

BIG Idea Animals, including people, have life needs and special physical features that can be classified according to certain characteristics	
Essential Questions	Knowledge and Skills (from VA State Standards for the First Grade)
■ What terms or words are specific to the work of a zoologist who studies animals? ■ What do animals need to live and grow? ■ What are some characteristics of animals that help them move, protect themselves, and survive? ■ What attributes or characteristics do scientist use to describe and classify animals? ■ What patterns of change emerge as different animals experience the seasons?	Know: 1.4.1 A zoologist uses his or her sense and tools to make observations about animals. 1.4.2 A zoologist classifies animals based on observable features. Do: 1.4.3 Analyze examples of various animal body coverings, body shapes, appendages, method of movement, and the concepts of wild versus tame. 1.4.4 Describe the life-needs of animals: food, water, shelter, and oxygen from air or water. 1.4.5 Infer types of animal homes (water or land) using physical characteristics of the animals. 1.4.6 Classify components of an animal's surroundings as living/non-living (including water, space, and shelter). 1.4.7 Compare and contrast the four seasons and predict how seasonal changes affect animals in terms of when and why animals migrate, hibernate, change their behavior, and change body covering. 1.4.8 Classify animals by where they live (their homes). 1.4.9 Classify and chart simple characteristics of animals. 1.4.10 Make and communicate observations of live animals, including people, about their needs, physical characteristics, and where they live.

Figure 5–1 Jenny Sue Flannagan, Virginia Beach City Public Schools, Virginia Beach, VA

Looking at animals and humans in this context of a big idea and essential questions instead of isolated facts, the students are able to make important connections—for example, "animals move to meet their needs." Thus movement of animals is seen as something animals and humans do to survive, and how they move can be a way to classify or put them into groups (e.g., two legs, four legs, or no legs; wings or no wings). This way, they begin to see classification as having set characteristics. They then can begin to recognize in later grades the overarching, unifying concept of adaptation.

Science Curriculum Topic Study

Not all districts are fortunate enough to have a person or department to help teachers move in this coherent direction; however, their new tools and resources coming into science education may help. Page Keeley, Senior Program Director for the Maine Mathematics and Science Alliance, has, with funding from the National Science Foundation, developed an effective tool for "unpacking" all of this for teachers and districts. It is called *Science Curriculum Topic Study* (Corwin 2005). This research-based process helps to improve teachers' understanding of science content, identify and clarify the "big ideas," and identify potential learning difficulties and misconceptions associated with a topic.

Page Keeley was a Presidential Award winning classroom science teacher before her move to the Alliance. She knows first hand how difficult and time consuming this can be for teachers and districts. Knowing where to start is an even bigger barrier to this process. Therefore, *Science Curriculum Topic Study* provides a standards-based and research-informed process that builds teachers' content knowledge of the topics they teach, helps them examine instructional implications, unpacks concepts and ideas that are important to teach, identifies misconceptions and potential learning difficulties, and makes coherent connections across and within grade levels (Corwin 2005, 59–60).

> *Unifying Concepts:* Fundamental and comprehensive non-discipline-specific concepts that provide connections between content standards in science (e.g., models, systems, patterns, change).
>
> *Big Ideas:* Generalizations, laws, theories, principles, or broad ideas that show relationships among concepts. Big ideas are the essential understandings that often cut across grade spans and information adult literacy (e.g., organisms depend on other organisms for their needs).
>
> *Concepts:* Mental constructs made up of one to three words that can be broad or topic specific. Even though factual knowledge may evolve and change, concepts remain universal and timeless. Concepts can begin with very basic ideas and culminate in sophisticated understanding. Students refine and enhance their thinking about concepts over the course of their K–12 experience (e.g., motion, adaptation, ecosystems, weathering).

Subconcepts: Concepts broken down into more specific mental constructs (e.g., horizontal motion, behavioral adaptation, lunar eclipse).

Specific Ideas: Scientific statements about a concept or subconcept that give it meaning. Specific ideas provide specificity for a broad local, state, or national learning goals (e.g., a rock is composed of different combinations of minerals).

Facts and Terminology: Definitions, formulas, fragments of specific knowledge, and technical vocabulary. While certain facts and terminology are necessary, when taught and learned in isolation they are less likely to contribute to conceptual understanding (e.g., density equals mass divided by volume; atoms are made up or protons, neutrons, and electrons).

How Can a District Use Curriculum Topic Study (CTS) to Bring Curriculum Coherence and Articulation?

Curriculum Topic Study (CTS) has been gaining in popularity across the science education community. It provides a tool to help districts look at their curricula and standards in a cohesive way. It helps by giving teachers a schema for breaking down ("unpacking") a topic, as well as "building up" into big ideas. By examining the concepts and ideas in a topic and considering recommendations from the standards and research on student learning, teachers can lay out a complete picture of the curriculum. It helps them to think of the flow of ideas to determine:

- The important core set of ideas students should learn, ranging from specific facts, terminology, and ideas to broad concepts, "big ideas," and unifying themes

- The major connections among ideas both within the content domain, across content domains, and across disciplines

- Cross-cutting processes and understandings to inquiry and technological design, the nature and history of science, and personal and social perspectives of science and technology

- Important prerequisites leading to increasing sophistication, by which students eventually come to understand important ideas in science from one grade level to the next and within grade levels (Corwin 2005, 62).

These are actually the pieces to the puzzle that will come together to help teachers see their district's curricula as a whole and not a set of disjointed grade-level expectations.

Effective teachers of science will understand the topics of their grade level. Those who are not effective are looking at the teaching of science as simply teaching ponds, butterflies, or dinosaurs, which are the themes or the stories of science. Effective teachers of science will use them; however, they will use them to develop, practice, and apply the big ideas and skills to get at the necessary content. They might use dinosaurs as the context, but it will not just be to give students facts and vocabulary—it will be to develop interrelated ideas and skills about changes in life forms and environment over time.

Whatever method a district uses to look closer at their curricula for coherence and alignment, they must not look at it through the lens of a "check-off" list of their state and district standards. Standards are important, but to get at the heart of developing scientifically literate students, teachers need to weave an interconnected web of understanding. For more reading and information about CTS, visit: www.curriculumtopicstudy.org

Deepening Teacher Content Knowledge

While visiting with a district curriculum superintendent she ask me what are some ways to help with the overarching problem of elementary teachers not having enough content knowledge to feel comfortable teaching science. It was not a simple question to answer. Therefore I said, "First of all, you have to provide purposeful, efficient, and effective professional development to deepen both your teachers' content and pedagogical knowledge. Not the one-time workshop after school, but sustained efforts giving teachers time to learn this new knowledge. Then provide mentoring and coaching to help them transform their classroom practice reflecting this new knowledge."

In *Taking Science to School* (NRC 2006), one of the key recommendations is that teachers to deepen their science content knowledge. "Professional development should be rooted in the science that teachers teach and should include opportunities to learn about science, about current research on how children learn science, and about how to teach science" (NRC 2006, ES-5). *Looking Inside the Classroom* backs up this recommendation (Horizon Research, Inc. 2003) by explaining what transpires in the nation's classrooms, and the factors that shape instruction in mathematics and science. The study points out that without question, teachers need to have sufficient knowledge of the mathematics/science content they are responsible for teaching. However, teacher content knowledge is not sufficient preparation for high-quality instruction. Teachers also need expertise in helping students develop an understanding of that content, including knowing how to determine what a particular student or group of students is thinking about those ideas, and how the available instruction materials can be used to help students deepen their understanding.

We now know (and research and studies are telling us) there is a national shift toward looking at the content knowledge that elementary teachers need. The NRC research in *How People Learn* (Bransford, Brown, and Cocking 1999) has helped to raise this awareness among educators and policy makers. They point out that the difference between novice and expert teachers is that the former:

- Know the structure of the knowledge in their disciplines.

- Know the conceptual barriers that are likely to hinder learning.

- Have well-organized knowledge of concepts and inquiry procedures and problem-solving strategies (based on pedagogical content knowledge).

If you are a classroom teacher or a professional development provider and you want to dig deeper into the content, there are some tools available to help (however, this does not replace formal science content coursework):

- *Curriculum Topic Study* (CTS) provides avenues and reading references to help teachers gain content knowledge. It does this by providing a systematic way for teachers to identify relevant grade-level content and increase their knowledge of the science ideas as well as understand how the knowledge is structured. Many district elementary science programs are using CTS to help enhance and identify what they don't know. By using the CTS guide and the optional content reading supplements on the CTS website (www.curriculumtopicstudy.org) teachers will be well on their way to helping to solve the problem.

- National Science Teachers Association (NSTA), the largest professional science teachers' organization, has recognized this as a growing concern. They offer many excellent resources to help elementary teachers deepen their content knowledge, one of which is a set of very popular books called *Stop Faking It! Finally Understanding Science So You Can Teach It* (Robertson, W. NSTA). Each book Focuses on a particular concept, such as air, water, and weather; force and motion; light; etc. Although they are listed as for grades 5–12, they can be used effectively in professional development experiences or study groups.

- These and other books published by NSTA are connected to the website called SciLinks. This central location helps teachers avoid searching hundreds of science websites to locate the best sources for more information on a given topic. You simply go into the URL (www.scilinks.org) and type the keyword code that is found by the logo on the book's page. You will then receive an annotated listing of as many as fifteen web pages, all of which have gone through an extensive review process that will help you understand the content. Try it with the concept of light and the topic of refraction; go to the website and type in the code SFL02 to view examples of content articles.

- Another effort by the National Science Teachers Association is their Learning Center. NSTA is creating a scalable e-Professional Development (e-PD) portal that will allow educators to utilize a comprehensive systems-based approach to their professional development. They have developed 26–30 comprehensive online learning experiences for K–12 science teachers focusing on fun, interactive science content learning experiences delivered through a state-of-the-art e-Professional Development portal.

- The Learning Center will be home base for science teachers and school systems in search of high-quality science content specifically addressing their individual needs and their system's professional development requirements. Educators are able to diagnose their needs and gain access to a variety of professional development resources and opportunities aligned to standards and the grade bands they teach. Personalized tools within the Learning Center, such as *My PD Plan and Portfolio, My Library, My Calendar,* and *My Transcript,* will allow educators to manage, track, document, and certify their professional development growth over a period of time. The beta launch of the NSTA Learning Center and all the resources below are available at *http://learningcenter.nsta.org.* You may view a 7-

minute multimedia overview of the NSTA Learning Center by going to: http://institute.nsta.org/learningcenter/flashdemo/index.html.

- As of spring 2007 there are more than 1,400 professional development resources and opportunities available within the Learning Center, with 35 percent available for free or less than $1.00. You do not need to be a member of NSTA to access the NSTA Learning Center, but members receive member discounts and/or free access to many resources. Professional development resources such as NSTA e-Books, e-Book Chapters, Journal Articles, Web Seminars, Symposia, SciGuides, Science Objects, and SciPacks are all available within the NSTA Learning Center.

- NSTA SciPacks are 5–10 hour-long, discrete, online learning experiences to assist educators in understanding the science content they teach. SciPacks are based on the national science standards and are accessible anytime, anywhere. The basic feature common to all SciPacks is a set of three to five Science Objects, each with embedded simulations and related follow-up questions. In addition to the free Science Objects, each SciPack contains a pedagogical section that provides the teaching context of the content. This part of the SciPack will be designed to help them recognize the level of sophistication appropriate for their students, identify or diagnose students' misconceptions, and employ strategies that are most effective for the particular ideas they teach. Each SciPack also provides individualized email support from a Content Wizard and concludes with a graded assessment that if passed, allows a teacher to print a "certificate" demonstrating mastery understanding of the content addressed.

Other efforts to improve and deepen teachers' content knowledge and add just-in-time resources right at their fingertips are:

- **NSTA SciGuides** are online, thematically based packages of pre-evaluated and standards-aligned web-accessible classroom resources for science teachers to use in their classroom. Each SciGuide consists of a library of approximately 100 web pages vetted against eight educational rubrics. Each SciGuide provides a brief content background description for the educator and links to the web-based resources. Each SciGuide has a set of tools to assist educators in implementing the web-based resources into their classroom with lesson plans, media vignettes, and samples of student work illustrating lesson outcomes.

- **NSTA Symposia** experiences are face-to-face workshops that provide follow-up online learning opportunities, such as live web seminars and asynchronous threaded discussion. The content of Symposia is delivered in partnership with

NASA, NOAA, FDA, NSF, and NSTA Press authors, with offerings in STEM-related content areas.

- **NSTA Web Seminars** are live, professional development experiences that allow participants to interact with nationally acclaimed experts, scientists, engineers, and education specialists from NSTA government partners such as NASA, NOAA, NSF, FDA—all from the convenience of a desktop computer! Educators use their browser to mark up and annotate presenter's slides or share desktop applications, in addition to engaging in chat with others and answering poll questions. Seminars are archived and available for viewing after the live event. Agency-sponsored web seminars are free and create learning opportunities for those unable to attend face-to-face opportunities.

- The National Science Digital Library (NSDL at www.nsdl.org), funded by NSF, provides research-based content to teachers for free. This same site can also be used for student research. NSDL lists resources and articles by reputable sources that are organized under broad umbrellas. There are also web seminars for teachers to attend around topics to help broaden their content knowledge.

Managing Inquiry-Based Learning

Mr. Hallock points out in Voices from the World many of the elements we have been discussing, but two of which we have not focused on are materials management and cooperative learning strategies, both of which go together to support inquiry-based science instruction.

You Need the Stuff to Teach Hands-on Science

Mr. Hallock's district and others around the country provide materials for their elementary science programs. This district has made elementary science a priority and the materials kits are delivered to every teacher from a central distribution center. These material resource centers can be found in some large districts across the country. To learn more about these resource centers, visit the Association of Materials Centers website www.kitsupport.org.

Many districts provide materials kits that are intended to last for the entire year, with a teacher or a school leader responsible for turning in the replenishment list at the end of the year. Whichever way the materials are delivered or supplied to the teacher, the main point is that to be an effective teacher of science you have to have the materials to do the hands-on investigations. You might find pockets of teachers who gather their own materials and are still very effective, but most of the time the teachers who rise to the top are those who have a strong support system.

Whether the district chooses to go with curriculum kits or modules that contain the materials, or uses textbooks combined with kits of materials, the materials are a must. We have discussed the importance of a coherent curriculum; however, this curriculum must be combined with the resources and materials for successful classroom implementation.

Just Putting the Students into Groups Does Not Guarantee Effectiveness

Frankie Troutman (see Voices from the Field) is a highly effective kindergarten teacher who is passionate and knowledgeable about the teaching of primary science. She is asked to deliver professional development seminars all over the country and knows that materials are not enough to be effective in executing an inquiry-based investigation. She therefore stresses cooperative learning. Science educators, because they encourage teachers to have students work in groups for their investigations and projects, have embraced cooperative learning techniques.

What is Cooperative Learning?

Cooperation is working together to accomplish shared goals. Within cooperative activities, individuals seek outcomes that are beneficial to themselves and beneficial to all other group members. *Cooperative learning* is the instructional use of small groups so that students work together to maximize their own and each other's learning. It is a successful teaching strategy in which small teams, each with students of different levels of ability, use a variety of learning activities to improve their understanding of a subject. Each member of a team is responsible not only for learning what is taught but also for helping teammates learn, thus creating an atmosphere of achievement. Students work through the activity until all group members successfully understand and complete it.

These cooperative efforts result in participants striving for mutual benefit so that all group members:

- Gain from each other's efforts. (Your success benefits me and my success benefits you.)

- Recognize that all group members share a common fate. (We all sink or swim together here.)

- Know that one's performance is mutually caused by oneself and one's team members. (We cannot do it without you.)

- Feel proud and jointly celebrate when a group member is recognized for achievement. (We all congratulate you on your accomplishment!).

There are a number of key elements that set cooperative learning apart from other grouping techniques (Cochran 1989, Johnson and Johnson 1999). These elements include the following:

- Heterogeneous grouping (mixing levels of student abilities especially ELLs)

- Positive interdependence (sinking or swimming together)

- Face-to-face supportive interaction

- Individual accountability (requiring each group member to contribute to the group's achievement of its goals; typically each member is assigned a specific role to perform in the group)

- Interpersonal and small group skills (communication, trust, leadership, decision making, and conflict resolution)

- Group processing (reflecting on how well the team is functioning and how it can function even better)

In a classroom of an effective teacher you will find these strategies employed, particularly during investigations. However, these same cooperative-learning strategies can be used throughout all subject areas and are not just for science instruction.

Summary Thoughts

Designing and delivering effective science instruction takes a coherent and aligned curriculum designed around the big ideas of science. This curriculum must be strategically built in order not to teach lots of pieces of science knowledge. To deliver this curriculum effectively teachers need to deepen their content and pedagogical knowledge. And for this curriculum to be effectively delivered in the classroom it needs to be supported with the appropriate tools and materials. Teachers cannot just put students into groups to have them complete activities and think they will be successful. Grouping and group skills must be specially taught by the teacher to guarantee success of all the group members.

References

Ball, Debra, and D. Cohen. 1996. "Reform By the Book: What Is— or Might Be—the Role of Curriculum Materials in Teacher Learning and Instructional Reform?" *Educational Researcher* 25 (9): 6–8.

Bransford, John, A. Brown, and R. Cocking, Editors. 1999. *How People Learn: Brain, Mind, Experience, and School.* Washington, DC: National Academy Press.

Duschl, Richard, H. Schweingruber, and A. Shouse, Editors. 2006. *Taking Science to School: Learning and Teaching Science in Grades K–8.* Washington, DC: National Academy Press.

Duschl, Richard. 1990. *Restructuring Science Education: The Importance of Theories and Their Development.* New York: Teachers College Press.

Hill, Jane, and K. Flynn. 2006. *Classroom Instruction that Works with English Language Learners.* Alexandria, VA: Association for Supervision and Curriculum Development.

Johnson, David, and R. Johnson. 1993. *Cooperation in the Classroom,* Sixth Edition. Edina, MN: Interaction Book Company.

National Science Resources Center. 1997. *Science for All Children*, Washington, DC: National Academy Press.

Robertson, William. 2006. *Stop Faking It! Finally Understanding Science So You Can Teach It.* Arlington, VA: National Science Teachers Association Press.

Weiss, I, J. Pasley, P. Smith, E. Banilower, and D. Heck. *Looking Inside the Classroom Study.* 2003. Chapel Hill, NC: Horizon Research, Inc.

Supporting All Learners

"Three principles from brain research: emotional safety, appropriate challenges, and self constructed meaning suggest that a one-size-fits-all approach to classroom instruction teaching is ineffective for most students and harmful to some."
—Carol Ann Tomlinson, *Teach Me, Teach My Brain—A Call for Differentiated Classrooms*

Many years ago, when I was a very young second-grade teacher, I had a special needs student named John. He came to me reading at a low first-grade level, could barely write his name, and because of a cleft palate, his speech was severely impaired. The year before, the teacher lounge talk was all about how John just needed to be put in a special class because he was "different," disruptive to the other learners, required too much attention, didn't want to learn, and would not stay in his seat. I learned all this was true within the first week, but I also learned that he had a deep affection for animals. In my classroom he found paradise, for he was surrounded by guinea pigs, a pair of parakeets, and a big white rabbit, which was allowed to run free most of the time. John had difficulties to overcome, but I found that he made progress by learning about these animals, writing about them, and becoming the classroom manager of their care and feeding. The context for teaching all the basics to John became science experiences. This is a Cinderella story because years later I ran into John and learned he went on to become a veterinarian. John had not fit the mold; therefore, he had been labeled "different." It was not me who turned John around; it was that he discovered science and it turned him on.

Children want and need to learn about the world around them. They want to know how things work and what makes them run. With the mounting pressures to get all students to read at grade level, sometimes reading and math are the only subjects they experience. True, the classrooms of today have changed, and the requirement to reach all learners provides many more pressures and barriers. However, the research is showing, like John showed, that science just might be the spark to ignite the desire to learn and, in some cases, where there are many second language learners, kids are able to learn and practice speaking English in a safe, interesting and motivating context . In this chapter we will explore the importance of providing science for all learners.

Once Separated, Now Included

After the U.S. census in 2000 it was estimated that nine million children between the ages of five and seven speak a language other than English at home, and many of these do not speak English well. More than half of these children come to preschool and kindergarten in order to learn to speak and read English. If they do not get the help in their early years of elementary school they will more than likely become another drop-out in high school.

At one time the English Language Learner (ELL), or English Learners (EL), belonged to the English as a Second Language (ESOL) staff, but now, due to the changing laws and policies, they are in every classroom across the nation. This makes the role of teaching in the elementary classroom, where most teachers have not been trained to handle ELLs, much more challenging. There are strategies that can be used for helping ELLs learn science, but most of all the teacher's attitude and effective teaching of science will make the difference to these and all students.

Lucille Barrera is an effective teacher of science who has moved into the district role of coaching and providing professional development for others. She offers the following strategies for teaching science to English learners:

VOICE FROM THE FIELD

My experience has been if teachers feel they can be effective at reaching all their students, then they will be or will gain the skills needed to become effective. The teacher must have a firm belief in and a commitment to the concept that all students can learn science. Part is the emotional involvement when confronted with second language learners is looking at them as "different." They are not different—they just require some different strategies to insure they have access to this new knowledge.

—*Lucille Barrera, Elementary Science Specialist for Houston Independent School District, Huston, Texas*

- Introduce and explain all new science terminology, technical terms, and concepts.
- Keep a science Word Wall in your classroom.
- Provide Spanish language textbooks and support materials whenever possible.
- Note English/Spanish cognates whenever possible.
- Provide context clues by using gestures or actions to convey meaning.
- Provide bilingual support for content materials, including translations of text.
- Label your science equipment with English and Spanish names.
- State and write learning objectives.
- Keep language simple.
- Use hands-on and inquiry-based activities and cooperative learning groups that are of mixed ability and language.
- Provide thematic units with culturally relevant material.
- Pair-share read all material to help the English learner gain access to the language.
- Have students keep a science notebook, especially for noting new vocabulary.
- Read orally and have students follow along.
- Allow more wait time to enable students to process and respond to verbal and written questions.
- Modify assessment by decreasing language demands and use performance-based assessments by allowing native language usage or drawings.

New Research and Strategies Emerge Every Year

The influx of English Language Learners in the mainstream classrooms has moved the way teachers teach, from "just talking" to their students to now having to think about how they are going to accommodate for all the different language speakers in the classroom. Furthermore no two ELLs have the same amount of grounding in their native language, or are at the same stage of English language acquisition.

Over the past few years the staff members at Mid-continent Research for Education and Learning (McREL) have worked with mainstream teachers in small rural districts in Wyoming, training them on instructional strategies for ELLs. In the course of this training they turned to *Classroom Instruction That Works* (Marzano, Pickering, and Pollock 2001) and found the strategies recommended through this work were the same ones some ELL specialists had been using as well (Hill and Flynn 2006).

The nine instructional strategies presented by Marzano, Pickering, and Pollock that are most likely to improve student achievement across all content areas and across all grade levels are:

1. Identifying similarities and differences

2. Summarizing and note-taking

3. Reinforcing effort and providing recognition

4. Homework and practice

5. Nonlinguistic representations

6 Cooperative learning

7. Setting objectives and providing feedback

8. Generating and testing hypotheses

9. Cues, questions, and advance organizers

The following is an overview of the research behind these strategies as well as some practical applications for the classroom.

1. Identifying Similarities and Differences

The ability to break a concept into its similar and dissimilar characteristics allows students to understand (and often solve) complex problems by analyzing them in a simpler way. Teachers can either directly present similarities and differences, accompanied by deep discussion and inquiry, or simply ask students to identify similarities and differences on their own. While teacher-directed activities focus on identifying specific items, research shows that student-directed activities encourage variation and broaden understanding. Research also notes that graphic forms are a good way to represent similarities and differences.

Applications:

- Use Venn diagrams or charts to compare and classify items.
- Engage students in comparing, classifying, and creating metaphors and analogies.

2. Summarizing and Note-Taking

These skills promote greater comprehension by asking students to analyze a subject to expose what's essential and then put it in their own words. According to research, this requires substituting, deleting, and keeping some things and having an awareness of the basic structure of the information presented.

Applications:

- Provide a set of rules for creating a summary.

- When summarizing, ask students to question what is unclear, clarify those questions, and then predict what will happen next in the text.

Research shows that taking more notes is better than fewer notes, though verbatim note-taking is ineffective because it does not allow time to process the information. Teachers should encourage and give time for review and revision of notes; notes can be the best study guides for tests.

Applications:

- Use teacher-prepared notes.

- Stick to a consistent format for notes, although students can refine the notes as necessary.

3. Reinforcing Effort and Providing Recognition

Effort and recognition speak to the attitudes and beliefs of students, and teachers must show the connection between effort and achievement. Research shows that although not all students realize the importance of effort, they can learn to change their beliefs to emphasize effort.

Applications:

- Share stories about people who succeeded by not giving up.

- Have students keep a log of their weekly efforts and achievements, reflect on it periodically, and even mathematically analyze the data.

According to research, recognition is most effective if it is contingent on the achievement of a certain standard. Also, symbolic recognition works better than tangible rewards.

Applications:

- Find ways to personalize recognition. Give awards for individual accomplishments.

- "Pause, Prompt, Praise." If a student is struggling, pause to discuss the problem, then prompt with specific suggestions to help her improve; if the student's performance improves as a result, offer praise.

4. Homework and Practice

Homework provides students with the opportunity to extend their learning outside the classroom. However, research shows that the amount of homework assigned should vary by grade level and that parent involvement should be minimal. Teachers should explain the purpose of homework to both the student and the parent or guardian, and teachers should try to give feedback on all homework assigned.

Applications:

- Establish a homework policy with advice—such as keeping a consistent schedule, setting, and time limit—that parents and students may not have considered.
- Tell students if homework is for practice or preparation for upcoming units.
- Maximize the effectiveness of feedback by varying the way it is delivered.

Research shows that students should adapt skills while they're learning them. Speed and accuracy are key indicators of the effectiveness of practice.

Applications:

- Assign timed quizzes for homework and have students report on their speed and accuracy.
- Focus practice on difficult concepts and set aside time to accommodate practice periods.

5. Nonlinguistic Representations

According to research, knowledge is stored in two forms: linguistic and visual. The more students use both forms in the classroom, the more opportunity they have to achieve. Recently, use of nonlinguistic representation has proven to not only stimulate but also increase brain activity.

Applications:

- Incorporate words and images using symbols to represent relationships.
- Use physical models and physical movement to represent information.

6. Cooperative Learning

Research shows that organizing students into cooperative groups yields a positive effect on overall learning. When applying cooperative learning strategies, keep groups small and don't overuse this strategy-be systematic and consistent in your approach.

Applications:

- When grouping students, consider a variety of criteria, such as common experiences or interests.

- Vary group sizes and objectives.

- Design group work around the core components of cooperative learning—positive interdependence, group processing, and appropriate use of social skills, face-to-face interaction, and individual and group accountability.

7. Setting Objectives and Providing Feedback

Setting objectives can provide students with direction for their learning. Goals should not be too specific; they should be easily adaptable to students' own objectives.

Applications:

- Set a core goal for a unit, and then encourage students to personalize that goal by identifying areas of interest to them. Questions like "I want to know" and "I want to know more about . . . " get students thinking about their interests and actively involved in the goal-setting process.

- Use contracts to outline the specific goals that students must attain and the grade they will receive if they meet those goals.

Research shows that feedback generally produces positive results. Teachers can never give too much; however, they should manage the form that feedback takes.

Applications:

- Make sure feedback is corrective in nature; tell students how they did in relation to specific levels of knowledge. Rubrics are a great way to do this.

- Keep feedback timely and specific.

- Encourage students to lead feedback sessions.

8. Generating and Testing Hypotheses

Research shows that a deductive approach (using a general rule to make a prediction) to this strategy works best. Whether a hypothesis is induced or deduced, students should clearly explain their hypotheses and conclusions.

Applications:

- Ask students to predict what would happen if an aspect of a familiar system, such as the government or transportation, were changed.

- Ask students to build something using limited resources. This task generates questions and hypotheses about what may or may not work.

9. Cues, Questions, and Advance Organizers

Cues, questions, and advance organizers help students use what they already know about a topic to enhance further learning. Research shows that these tools should be highly analytical, should focus on what is important, and are most effective when presented before a learning experience.

Applications:

- Pause briefly after asking a question. Doing so will increase the depth of your students' answers.

- Vary the style of advance organizer used: Tell a story, skim a text, or create a graphic image. There are many ways to expose students to information before they "learn" it.

To help students to learn a new language is not only difficult; it is time consuming. To help students learn content in a new language, we must use clear and concise articulation, make eye contact, use visuals, employ gestures/body movement/pantomime, use shorter and simpler sentences at a slower rate, use high-frequency vocabulary, and eliminate idiomatic expressions. We also have to model, scaffold, access, and activate students' prior knowledge; provide cooperative learning activities; and differentiate instruction. Making such accommodations helps provide better instruction for ELLs and all students. (Hill and Flynn 2006, 2).

Differentiated Instruction

Differentiating instruction means creating multiple paths so that students of different abilities, interest, or learning needs experience equally appropriate ways to absorb, use, develop and present concepts as a part of the daily learning process. It allows students to take greater responsibility and ownership for their own learning, and provides opportunities for peer teaching and cooperative learning. No single classroom will have the same homogeneous students; more than likely one classroom will have students who can read and comprehend as well as most college learners; students who can barely decode words, comprehend meaning, or apply basic information; and students who fall somewhere between these extremes. There simply is no single learning template for any classroom. When it comes to teaching science, the same holds true: some can read, comprehend, and work together, while others will not. Therefore, in order to foster continual growth, a one-size-fits-all model of instruction makes little sense. Rather in some cases, using differentiated instruction seems a better solution for meeting the academic diversity.

What Differentiation Is, and Is Not

A differentiated classroom offers a variety of learning options designed to tap into different readiness levels, interests, and learning profiles. In a differentiated class, the teacher uses:

- A variety of ways for students to explore curriculum content

- A variety of sense-making activities or processes through which students can come to understand and "own" information and ideas

- A variety of options through which students can demonstrate or exhibit what they have learned.

A class is not differentiated when assignments are the same for all learners and the adjustments consist of varying the level of difficulty of questions for certain students, grading some students harder than others, or letting students who finish early play games for enrichment. It is not appropriate to have more advanced learners do extra science experiments and problems, extra reports, or after completing their "regular" work be given extension assignments. Asking students to do more of what they already know is hollow. Asking them to do "the regular work, plus" inevitably seems punitive to them (Tomlinson 1995).

Four Characteristics Shape Teaching and Learning in an Effective Differentiated Classroom

1. *Instruction is concept focused and principle driven.* All students have the opportunity to explore and apply the key concepts of the subject being studied. All students come to understand the key principles on which the study is based. Such instruction enables struggling learners to grasp and use powerful ideas and, at the same time, encourages advanced learners to expand their understanding and application of the key concepts and principles. Such instruction stresses understanding or sense-making rather than retention and regurgitation of fragmented bits of information. Concept-based and principle-driven instruction invites teachers to provide varied learning options. A "coverage-based" curriculum may cause a teacher to feel compelled to see that all students do the same work. In the former, all students have the opportunity to explore meaningful ideas through a variety of avenues and approaches.

2. *On-going assessment of student readiness and growth are built into the curriculum.* Teachers do not assume that all students need a given task or segment of study, but continuously assess student readiness and interest, providing support when students need additional instruction and guidance, and extending student exploration when indications are that a student or group of students is ready to move ahead.

3. *Flexible grouping is consistently used.* In a differentiated class, students work in many patterns. Sometimes they work alone, sometimes in pairs, sometimes in groups. Sometimes tasks are readiness-based, sometimes interest-based, sometimes constructed to match learning style, and sometimes a combination of these. In a differentiated classroom, whole-group instruction may also be used for introducing new ideas, when planning, and for sharing learning outcomes.

4. *Students are active explorers. Teachers guide the exploration.* Because varied activities often occur simultaneously in a differentiated classroom, the teacher works more as a guide or facilitator of learning than as a dispenser of information. Not only does such student-centeredness give students more ownership of their learning, but it also facilitates the important adolescent learning goal of growing independence in thought, planning, and evaluation. Implicit in such instruction is (1) goal-setting shared by teacher and student based on student readiness, interest, and learning profile, and (2) assessment predicated on student growth and goal attainment (Tomlinson 1995a).

Differentiation Instruction in the Science Classroom

Science instruction can be differentiated to allow students to explore topics of interest, expand their research skills, and receive instruction on discrete science and inquiry skills. Figure 6–1 offers a variety of strategies that can be used.

Figure 6–1   *Strategies for Differentiation in Science, J. Vasquez*

Strategy	Focus of Differentiation	Definition	Example
Tiered Assessments	Readiness	Tiered assessments are designed to instruct students on essential skill that are provided at different levels of complexity, abstractness, and open-endedness. The curriculum content and objective(s) are the same, but the process and/or product are varied according to the student's level of readiness.	Some students are provided with direct instruction on the characteristics of living vs. non-living things, and are given guidance in identifying members of both groups. Other students work in teams to identify members of both groups and come up with original examples.
Compacting	Readiness	Compacting is the process of adjusting instruction to account for prior student mastery of learning objectives. Compacting involves a three-step process: (1) assess the student to determine his/her level of knowledge on the material to be studied and determine what he/she still needs to master; (2) create plans for what the student needs to know, and excuse the student from studying what he/she already knows; and (3) create plans for freed-up time to be spent in enriched or accelerated study.	In a science class students who already know a topic are given a lab assignment in which they must develop and test hypotheses related to the topic, while other students are given more direct instruction on the concept.

continued

Figure 6–1 *Strategies for Differentiation in Science, J. Vasquez*

Strategy	Focus of Differentiation	Definition	Example
Interest Centers	Readiness Interest	Interest centers are set up so that learning experiences are directed toward a specific learner interest. Allow students to choose a topic that can be motivating to them.	Interest centers can focus on specific topics in Earth Science, such as classifying rocks or doing research on a particular kind of rock.
Flexible Grouping*	Readiness Interest Learning Profile	Students work as part of many different groups depending on the task and/or content. Sometimes students are placed in groups based on readiness; other times they are placed based on interest and/or learning profile. Groups can either be assigned by the teacher or chosen by the students. Students can be assigned purposefully to a group or assigned randomly. This strategy allows students to work with a wide variety of peers and keeps them from being labeled as advanced or struggling.	The teacher may assign groups based on student characteristics for an investigation in which each group member must take on a specific role. For example, a student who is a strong writer might take notes for the group, while a student who enjoys public speaking might present the group's findings. Students may choose their own groups for another investigation in which they will explore a new problem or investigation.

continued

Figure 6–1 *Strategies for Differentiation in Science, J. Vasquez*

Strategy	Focus of Differentiation	Definition	Example
Learning Contracts	Readiness Learning Profile	Learning contracts begin with an agreement between the teacher and the student. The teacher specifies the necessary skills expected to be learned by the student and the required components of the assignment, while the student identifies methods for completing the tasks. This strategy (1) allows students to work at an appropriate pace; (2) can target learning styles; and (3) helps students work independently, learn planning skills, and eliminate unnecessary skill practice.	With the teacher's guidance, the student develops a plan for researching a particular topic.
Choice Boards	Readiness Interest Learning Profile	Choice boards are organizers that contain a variety of activities. Students can choose one or several activities to complete as they learn a skill or develop a product. Choice boards can be organized so that students are required to choose options that focus on several different skills.	Students are given a choice board that contains a list of possible activities they can complete. Perhaps they decide on density. They can have activities that include using a water table to explore properties of various objects, or they can read or do research on the Internet. The activities are based on the following learning styles: visual, auditory, kinesthetic, and tactile. Students must complete two activities from the board and must choose these activities from two different learning styles.

Providing for Gender Equity

Gender equity means *creating an educational climate that encourages males and females equally to develop, achieve, and learn.* As in the phrase, "A rising tide lifts all boats," gender equity is inclusive and promotes the full development of all students. It is not a zero-sum game, wherein one gender succeeds at the expense of the other. All students should be treated equitably in school, have equal encouragement to learn, have no limits on expectations placed on them due to gender, and have open options to learn all subjects and prepare for future education, jobs, and careers.

—*Dr. Dorothy J. T. Terman, former Science and Math Coordinator,*
Irvine Unified School District, Irvine, California

Gender bias can be defined as *attitudes and actions that stereotype or discriminate against a person on the basis of gender—whether intentional or not.* In the vast majority of cases, gender bias in education *is* unintentional. Gender bias is subtle and can consist of inadvertently assuming that a girl will not be interested in math or in auto-repair classes, steering boys to advanced science classes, or acknowledging the in-class contributions of boys more frequently than those of girls.

Gender-biased perceptions can lead to differential expectations for the behaviors or capabilities of boys and girls on the part of teachers and parents. We then may subtly behave differently toward boys and girls based on these perceptions. For example, teachers may praise a girl more for the appearance and organization of a written report than for its content, and may give more evaluative feedback to a boy on the content of a report than on its presentation. The way we act toward boys and girls may eventually influence their self-perceptions and aspirations regarding further education and career options, resulting in self-imposed limitations on their futures.

In fourth grade, the number of girls and boys who like math or science is about the same. But by eighth grade, twice as many boys as girls show an interest in these subjects. It is critical that classroom teachers encourage all students to develop and foster a love for science.

Dr. Terman offers the following advice:

An excellent source of gender-equitable teaching strategies is 'GESA: Generating Expectations for Student Achievement', a staff-development program created by Dolores A. Grayson and Mary D. Martin. GESA synthesizes the research on gender bias in the classroom and presents a variety of research-based instructional strategies that reduce bias and lead to improved achievement for students of both genders. Among the most effective strategies for improving gender equity in the classroom are:

- Providing equitable response opportunities for students
- Acknowledging student contributions and providing feedback
- Increasing wait time between asking a question and accepting student responses
- Asking higher-level questions
- Providing analytical feedback to students

Other effective strategies for encouraging girls (and boys) to equitably develop, learn, and achieve, are to invite role models to mentor students, take field trips to see real-world applications of learning, and participate in science fairs and other contests, such as the Sally Ride Science Toy Challenge, Science Olympiad, and the FIRST Robotics Competition. Many universities host Expanding Your Horizons conferences and Sally Ride Science Festivals that are fun and exciting ways for girls to be introduced to future career opportunities and possibilities.

Many resources and ideas for involvement of girls and boys in science can be found on Sally Ride's website: www.sallyridescience.com.

Summary Thoughts

Teaching is difficult enough, and No Child Left Behind (NCLB) calling for quality education and accountability for all children has pushed all the pressure points. Science is one of the great equalizers within the classroom. There is growing research about how it will help non-English speakers respond and learn not just the science content but learn to read and write with more proficiency. All students deserve to have access to quality science instruction and many of the strategies presented here will help teachers enhance their instruction to address all their students' learning styles. It is also good to notice many of the strategies and suggestions presented here are the very same strategies we have already discussed for quality science instruction, cooperative learning, learning centers, communication, scaffolding of learning, and hands-on learning, to point to just a few. Science is the great equalizer in the classroom. Students love it if only given the opportunity to learn.

References

Hill, Jane, and K. Flynn. 2006. *Classroom Instruction that Works with English Language Learners.* Alexandria, VA: Association for Supervision and Curriculum Development.

Marzano, Robert, D. Pickering, and J. Pollock. 2001. *Classroom Instruction That Works.* Alexandria, VA: Association for Supervision and Curriculum Development.

McIntyre, Ellen, A. Rosebery, and N.Gonzalez. 2001. *Classroom Diversity: Connecting Curriculum to Students' Lives.* Portsmouth, NH: Heinemann.

Jarrett, Denise. 1999. *The Inclusive Classroom: Teaching Mathematics and Science to English Language Learners.* Portland, OR: Northwest Regional Educational Laboratory.

Shaw, Jay. 2002. "Linguistically Responsive Science Teaching." *Electronic Magazine of Multicultural Education* [online], 4 (1). www.eastern.edu/publications/emme/2002spring/shaw.html

Tomlinson, Carol. 1995. *How to Differentiate Instruction in Mixed-ability Classrooms.* Alexandria, VA: Association for Supervision and Curriculum Development.

Tomlinson, Carol. 1999. *The Differentiated Classroom: Responding to the Needs of All Learners* Alexandria, VA: Association for Supervision and Curriculum Development.

CHAPTER 7

Administrative Support for Effective Elementary Science

Marc Tucker (2004) labels the conditions of the coherent instructional system. These are clear standards; high-quality examinations designed to assess whether the standards have been met, curriculum frameworks specifying what topics and concepts are to be taught at each grade level, and a standard required curriculum. Even if all these elements are in place without a supportive system to help teachers become effective, nothing will change. District-level and school-level administrators need to know and truly understand what it takes to provide quality science instruction for their students.

With all the pressures on teachers and administrators to raise achievement scores and be held accountable for reading and mathematics, science in many places has been moved to the back burner. However, all of this is going to change as No Child Left Behind moves to include science testing in the accountability of Average Yearly Progress (AYP). Some exemplary districts where science in the elementary schools has been a sustained priority are feeling the pressure but still managing to support effective teaching.

One such district is Mesa Public Schools, Mesa, Arizona, which has one of the longest running materials centers and provides science curricula, materials, and professional development support for every elementary teacher. Mesa is Arizona's largest school district with a diverse population of 74,000 students. Like all large districts, Mesa has continued to grow and spread out as its central core has become the home to its growing minority, largely Hispanic, population.

I sat down with Dr. Michael B. Cowan, Associate Superintendent to listen as he gave me a very candid and honest glimpse of the pressures surrounding the teaching of elementary science in today's climate. Michael has a unique lens with which to view science education, as he was a sixth-grade teacher, a district level science specialist, the Director of the Science and Social Studies Resource Center, and Director of Curriculum before assuming his present role three years ago. This wide variety of experiences has helped him view science instruction and support from many angles.

Michael, from your perspective, how has the teaching of elementary science changed over the past few years of your administrative leadership?

"Implementation of the expectations of NCLB has been a significant challenge for our teachers. The competition between subjects for instructional time is daunting. When time within the school day, with the required 90 to 120 minutes for reading followed by additional time for reading intervention, along with the push for math competency, science gets moved to the background in many instances. When teachers do teach science, as they are required by our district to do, many are compelled to have the students just read science literature books, and they don't engage the students in our hands-on kits we provide for them. That's not science instruction."

"I also see several new teachers coming into the classroom with the basic skills to develop student literacy in mathematics and reading; however, it seems they do not have the same level of skills or the knowledge base for developing literacy in science. The deficiency requires districts to build basic science instruction capacities. This is something we try to do at the district level, but the competition for time for professional development is scarce when so much pressure is on reading and math. We just don't help by giving this newer generation of teachers the skills necessary to teach science in an inquiry-oriented manner."

Do you think then that we should require more content knowledge in science for our prospective teachers?

"The simple answer is 'Yes.' Teacher education does not require pre-service teachers to have both the content and pedagogy they need to understand the basic components of science lessons. I do know there are some universities that are now requiring pre-service teachers to take more science content courses so that they at least have the basic understanding of science concepts needed to teach on or at a sixth-grade level. Unfortunately, they are few and far apart. If teachers are teaching about static electricity then they themselves have to feel comfortable understanding the difference between current and static electricity, positive and negative charge, etc. Science content instruction would equip them with at least the basics."

What do you say to pre-service teachers who says they do not ever want to teach intermediate and therefore they don't need to know as much science?

"Future elementary teachers, regardless of the grade levels they teach, should know how to appropriately teach science and be comfortable with the content of each lesson.

The job of universities or other teacher preparation institutions is to prepare our future teachers. This means they need to come with a basic understanding of all the content areas. They are generalists. It is essential that they have competencies in multiple content areas. If you are going to be a primary teacher, then you need to know basic foundational skills are needed in science to lay the foundation for building the concepts. If they are teaching about static electricity, for instance, then beginning experiences with magnets is needed to give students the concept of negative and positive, or a push and pull."

What about integrations of the curriculum? Is this possible in the current climate of NCLB?

"I think that a skilled teacher, in some cases, has an intuitive knowledge about the interconnectedness of science and other subject areas. The master teacher understands how to effectively integrate content from numerous subject areas to help students to be successful. It is difficult for the novice teacher to get his (or her) hands around real, appropriate integration. It requires a professional savvy in instruction, comfort with content, and flexibility of scheduling. Often, teachers must call upon both the science of effective teaching and the art of teaching to really integrate instruction."

"With the time and content pressures of NCLB facing teachers, one of the only ways for us to really include adequate instruction for science will be the integration of subjects. Science brings application and purpose to the learning in reading and mathematics. It can be accomplished, but making it a reality is challenging to say the least."

Now that science will be a tested core subject, how do you think things are going to change in the classroom?

"I think we are going to go forward to the past. What I mean is, if you look back 15 to 20 years ago, we had Project 2061, Science of All Americans Benchmarks, and then the National Science Education Standards. Within that time, many science education reform efforts were taking place and we were just beginning to see the fruits of our labors when NCLB came into being. We were required to sacrifice something to meet all the demands. I think with the new reports coming out on our new global economy and the needs for a knowledge-based, literate worker, things are going to change. They have to change. We will begin to 'right the curriculum ship' and, hopefully, go back to teaching a balanced curriculum for the education focused on the whole child."

"We traveled so far out there on the 'sea of accountability' with all the federal mandates that, in some cases, elementary schools were eliminating recess for more time-on-task for their students. This has been at the complete elimination of the time for children to explore and wonder. Science, in some cases, has become a mechanical function. It's not all about memorizing pre-set, academic vocabulary and isolated concepts. Science instruction, emphasizing inquiry and the manipulation of materials, should be an instituted aspect of the elementary school day."

So, do you see a danger in the testing of science as part of AYP?

"Accountability is not a bad word. We need to hold students and teachers accountable and implement ways for measuring their progress. My hope is that science does not become one of these content areas where the fourth-grade teacher is responsible for all the content and she or he teaches only that which is going to be tested. It can't be another 'fill in the blank' exam. If we use this type of exam, then it has to make the students stop and think about the answer and have some background understanding of the concept which is being tested."

In your vast experiences, when you walk into an elementary classroom and see a science lesson being taught, what indicators do you look for in a highly effective teacher?

"I look for the teacher's have a 'with-it-ness.' That's the innate ability to orchestrate a meaningful experience for students, ask the right questions at the right times, set up the experience appropriately, use materials to teach the concept, and help students learn how to form a testable hypothesis and communicate it to others. They know first of all the 'art of teaching.' These teachers also know and take the teachable moment. They know how to bridge to the other subjects and how not to isolate one content area, for they know they will loose out."

Since the principal is the curriculum leader of the school, how do we help them develop these highly effective teachers of science?

"In our district we hold the principals accountable for all the subject areas and it is our mission to help them, as some are not experts in quality science instruction, to know what this looks like. Principals are critical as they are the instructional leaders. We try to give our principals the tools they need so they know how to evaluate a quality science lesson. Plus, because we have a hands-on kit-based program for science, these principals will know which teachers are teaching science, and which are not. We also provide principal professional development throughout the course of the year, so they are familiar with both the processes and content expected during science instruction at each grade level."

We use to do a lot with cooperative learning to help with group management and accountability. Do you see any of this going on in the classroom and/or in professional development experiences?

"Once again, we are going to have to go backward to move forward. Many of the effective strategies we used in science education, cooperative learning, and even Madeline

Hunter's essential skills, have gone by the wayside for the 'quick-fix' of the month. We somehow forgot that these foundational educational practices were, and continue to be, sound educational practices. We need to give them time to become institutionalized. We need to analyze some of the strategies we used in the past. They need to come back into focus, now that science literacy is once again stepping into the spotlight."

Any thoughts about what the future holds for all the students you are responsible for helping in your district?

"I had the opportunity to go to China last year. We visited many schools and without going into great detail or analyzing who does and doesn't get a quality education in that country, I can sum it up with this way: They are so far ahead of us in the teaching of math and science. It is a funded emphasis, and instructional expectations for their students are set high. We have the most complex and viable education system in the world. We must give our students the opportunity to explore and learn science and mathematics. Students must be equipped with the ability to academically compete. Right now, in the current climate, we are not doing this as well as we should."

There are many districts where policy and administrative support has not wavered. As Dr. Cowan points out there are now new challenges to this support but even more urgency to try and find a way to provide a cohesive system of sustained teacher professional development and better preparation of new teachers so they will be prepared to teach science effectively. The key to having effective teachers teaching science is a well-informed and educated administration. Most elementary administrators and district-level administrators are not well versed in science education. They need to go through the preparation and mentoring on what effective practice in science looks like in order for any type of change to occur within the system. It is a bottom-up and top-down approach to supporting and sustaining science instruction.

Inside the Classroom

When an administrator walks into a classroom, how might he or she judge a quality lesson or an effective teacher of science? Surprisingly there were very few observation protocols designed just for science, particularly at the elementary level. In their study Looking Inside the Classroom: *A study of K-12 Mathematics and Science Education in the United States* (Weiss 2003), Horizon Research, Inc. provided a list of indicators that can prove valuable for designing an observation.

Figure 7–1

Indicators of Quality Science Instructionn

Quality of Lesson Design

- Resources available contribute to accomplishing the purpose of the instruction
- The design reflects careful planning and organization
- Strategies and activities reflect attention to students' preparedness and prior experience
- Strategies and activities reflect attention to issues of access, equity, and diversity
- The lesson incorporates tasks, roles, and interactions consistent with investigative science
- The design encourages collaboration among students
- The design provides adequate time and structure for sense-making
- The design provides adequate time and structure for wrap-up

Quality of Lesson Implementation

- Teacher appears confident in ability to teach science
- Teacher's classroom management enhances quality of lesson
- Pace is appropriate for developmental levels/needs of students
- Teacher is able to adjust instruction according to level of students' understanding
- Instructional strategies are consistent with investigative science
- Teacher's questioning enhances development of students' understanding/problem solving

Quality of Science Content

- Content is significant and worthwhile
- Content information is accurate
- Content is appropriate for developmental levels of students
- Teacher displays understanding of concepts
- Elements of abstraction are included when important
- Appropriate connections are made to other areas
- Students are intellectually engaged with important ideas
- Subject is portrayed as dynamic body of knowledge
- Degree of sense-making is appropriate for this lesson

Quality of Classroom Culture

- Climate is respectful of students' ideas, questions, and contributions
- Active participation of all is encouraged and valued
- Interactions reflect working relationship between teacher and students
- Interactions reflect working relationships among students
- Climate encourages students to generate ideas and questions
- Intellectual rigor, constructive criticism, and the challenging of ideas are evident

Figure 7–1 Indicators of Quality Science Instruction adapted from the NSF funded study: *Looking Inside the Classroom: A Study of K–12 Mathematics and Science Education in the United States.*

Administrative Support for Professional Learning Communities

As an organizational arrangement, the professional learning community is seen as a powerful staff development approach and a potent strategy for school change and improvement. Growing in popularity among science educators, this type of professional development is showing promise to help all teachers grow. For teachers who are novice teachers of science to have time to engage in professional conversations with effective teachers of science is worth much more than the one-time workshops and/or the make-and-take activities they sometime receive.

Research findings have confirmed professional learning communities can also raise academic achievement by improving instruction capacity in the classroom. Recent research shows that the kinds of professional development that improve instructional capacity display four critical characteristics. They are:

- Ongoing
- Embedded within context-specific needs of a particular setting
- Aligned with reform initiatives
- Grounded in collaborative, inquiry-based approach to learning

For these professional learning communities to be highly effective in science instruction they must move beyond process and integrate or focus on instructional content, beginning with literacy and science.

New Technologies Offer New Challenges and Opportunities

We are educating a generation of technology "natives" who have grown up with sophisticated communications and information technologies. This fact alone has helped to transform the way technology is being used and integrated into classroom instruction. Since the 1990s, school systems have invested heavily in Information Technology (IT), as a paper-based system does not make much sense to this generation of students. We have not seen the effectiveness of IT in classroom instruction other than in tutorials; however, with the number of students gaining access to technology, we will begin to see advances emerge in our nation's classrooms. These may include simulations, specialized laboratories, Web research, data collection, analysis projects based outside the school, and experiences and communications with experts or even other students for projects. Technology can be an effective tool for supporting the learning of science. The challenge becomes providing educators the professional development for using and integrating this way of teaching into their classroom.

Leaving an Entire Generation Behind

Research shows that the quality of a child's teacher is a key factor in closing the achievement gaps that exist today and ensuring that all students are prepared for success in today's society. Recent reports have pointed to this fact. K–12 elementary and secondary indicators clearly point to a lack of improvements in student achievement in mathematics and science. Average mathematics scores on national assessments rose during the 1990s and early 2000s; however, performance in science has not improved. There are far too many performance disparities in mathematics and science in disadvantaged populations, both urban and rural, where students lag far behind their peers. These disparities start as early as kindergarten, persisting across grades, and in most cases widen over time.

The Trends in International Math and Science Study (TIMSS) assessment's international comparisons between 1995 and 2003 showed some improvement for U.S. eighth-grade students in both math and science. This test measures mastery of curriculum-based knowledge and skills. However, scores for fourth graders generally remained flat over the same period. In 2003 the Program for International Student Assessment (PISA) test, which measure students' ability to apply scientific and mathematical concepts and skills, was administered to U.S. fifteen-year-olds. U.S. students scored below the international average. It should be noted that TIMSS included both developed and developing nations; the international averages for PISA are based on scores for the thirty Organization for Economic Co-operation and Development (OECD) countries, countries that are industrialized. The comparison of these two international tests begs the question: Are we teaching students how to think, or is it a matter of imparting knowledge and facts to our students so that they can pass the test?

We have focused on reading scores, math tests, and closing the "achievement gap" between social classes. It is not about leaving a fraction of children behind; it is now about leaving an entire generation of students behind—generations who will fail to make the grade in the global economy because they can't think their way through abstract problems, work in teams, distinguish good information from bad, or speak a language other than English. We need to bring what we teach and how we teach into the 21st century because right now we aim too low! Scientific literacy will be the key to the next workforce.

Conclusion

Many of the more than 2,300,000 elementary teachers walk into their classrooms every school day filled with hope, excitement, and a true commitment to making a difference in a child's life only to find a huge array of obstacles standing in their way. These classrooms are no longer filled with "Theodores" (the Beaver from the 1950s TV show *Leave It To Beaver.*) These classrooms are filled with children who come from diverse ethnic and social backgrounds and for many their primary language is not English. Many come from single-parent homes or are living with their grandparents. Many have parents who have to work, leaving them to become "latch key" children. The scenario of the child portrayed in the 1950s sitcom is long gone. Layered on all these challenges comes the new age of high accountability for all students. These students must pass the test with a set proficiency; it doesn't matter if they made huge gains in learning from the prior year. Not making the mark is failing, and the teacher is held accountable. One has to ask why they do it. There are many easier jobs out there. Over the years I've learned one important thing about teachers: they love children and value the job they do. Teachers find their challenge is not just finding ways to motivate their students, but finding ways that will not de-motivate them (in other words, turn them off!).

Effective teaching has proven to make a difference in student achievement; however, it cannot be just one teacher in the six or seven years students spend in elementary school. To raise achievement students must have consistent exposure to at least three effective teachers in a row. For teachers to be effective science instructors they need to have both content and pedagogical knowledge, actively engage their students in inquiry learning, use techniques that will develop students' higher-order thinking skills, understand and use cooperative learning strategies, be able to facilitate and manage hands-on learning activities, provide developmentally appropriate instruction that is relevant to their students' lives, accommodate for individual student needs (whether cultural, developmental, or cognitive), and while doing all this they must ensure all their students "pass the test." Elementary teachers are expected to be experts in all the curricular fields they are required to teach. They are not! To become experts they need to have sustained professional development, mentoring, and coaching because a majority of these teachers did not have the type of preparation in their pre-service experience needed to teach science effectively.

Science instruction in many elementary classrooms has become very content-driven, with students learning a laundry list of terms to pass the test. We want our students to have more than "terms" in their heads, or they will not have a love for science or a sense of wonder about the natural world. Rachel Carson, noted biologist and writer, says it best; although talking about parents and young children, the same advice can be given to elementary teachers:

> I sincerely believe that for the child, and for the parent seeking to guide him, it is not half so important to know as to feel. If facts are the seeds that later produce knowledge and wisdom, then the emotions and impressions of the senses are the fertile soil in which the seeds must grow. The years of early childhood are the time to prepare the soil . . . It is more important to pave the way for the child to want to know than to put him on a diet of facts he is not ready to assimilate. (Carson 1968)

America's competitive edge in this "flat world," its strength and versatility, all depends on an educational pipeline capable of producing a steady supply of young people well prepared in science and mathematics. Without preparing and supporting our elementary teachers to become effective teachers of science so that they can lay a firm foundation, and instill love of science and a sense of wonder in their students, we run the risk of raising a generation that is turned off and tuned out. They will not know how to think critically, make informed decisions based on their understanding of information, nor will they have a firm grasp of the knowledge necessary to advance into science, technology, engineering and mathematics (STEM) careers. They will not be able to produce the innovation and discovery necessary to sustain our nation's prosperity for the future. It sounds like clear warning, but it all begins in the classroom. If effective science teaching and learning is left behind, we leave this generation behind. It is a pipeline issue, and the pipeline begins when that child walks into the preschool or kindergarten to begin their life of formal learning.

References

Carson, Rachel. 1968. *The Sense of Wonder*. New York: Harper and Row.

Index

Generating Expectations for Student Achievement (GESA), 89–90
Graphic representations, 79, 81
Grayson, Dolores A., 89
Green, Stacey, 37, 40, 53
Group work. *See* Cooperative learning
Guided inquiry, 16, 17–18, *21*

H
Hallock, Michael, 35, 71, 72
Hands-on science activities, 2, 5, 6, 8
Harlen, Wynn, 45, 49, 50
Highly effective teachers, ix, x, 1–2
Highly qualified teachers, ix, x, 1–2
Homework, 81
Horizon Research, Inc., 3, 68, 96, *97*
Horsetmeyer, Kathy, 49
How People Learn (National Research Council), 8, 19, 41, 62, 68
"How" questions, 44–45, 46–47, 50–51
How Students Learn: Science in the Classroom (National Research Council), 6, 7, 30, 60
How Teaching Matters: Bringing the Classroom Back Into Discussions of Teacher Quality (Wenglinsky), 4
Hunter, Madeline, 95–96
Hypotheses, 83

I
Illustrations, in books, 35
Images, 79, 81
Important understandings. *See* Big ideas
Information Technology (IT), 98
Inquiry and the National Science Education Standards (National Research Council), 12, 14, 19
Inquiry-based teaching, x, 10–23
  cooperative learning in, 72–74
  elements of, 12
  examples of, 17–18, 20, *20–23*, 27–28
  5-E instruction model for, 19, 20, *20–23*
  implications of, 19–20

  importance of, 10
  materials management for, 71–72
  phases of, 14–18, *15*
  questions in, 45, 51
  teachers skilled in, 7–8, 11
Interest centers, *87*

K
Keeley, Page, ix–xi, 41, 65

L
Learning
  assessment for, 37–38
  cooperative, 5, 72–74, 82, 95–96
  evidence of, 44–47
  line of, 53, *54, 58*
  principles of, 19
Learning Center (National Science Teachers Association), 69–70
Learning contracts, *88*
Learning goals, 19, 82
Learning Science and the Science of Learning (Bybee), 13
Leaves, 38, 39, 41
Lesson design, quality of, *97*
Lesson implementation, quality of, *97*
Line of learning, 53, *54, 58*
Literacy development, science and, x, 25–36
  example of, 27–28
  notebooks for, 51–59, *54–58*
  research on, 28–30
  skills in, 26
  strategies for, 30, *31–33*
Long-term memory, 29
Looking Inside the Classroom (Horizon Research, Inc.), 68, 96, *97*
Lustick, D., 2

M
Magnets, 28–29, 30
Maine Mathematics and Science Alliance (MMSA), 12, 41, 65

Elizabeth
Faustyna